Reflections Through The Mist

Reflections Through the Mist

Based on and inspired by the memoir of Jean Etheridge 1917–2013

David Muir

Hoddamdale Books

Author's Note: What follows is based on actual occurrences and real people. Although some material has been added for fictional purposes, the work can be regarded in its essence as fact.

This is a work of creative non-fiction based on the life experiences and recollections of the author's mother. A number of characters, places and incidents are the product of the author's imagination and are used fictitiously for narrative purposes; any resemblance of such characters to any person, living or dead, is entirely coincidental.

The cover is a photograph of the author's mother, taken in the late 1930s when she was in her twenties, set against a background of part of the village in Scotland where the Muir family comes from.

ISBN 9798862546996

This book is dedicated to my mother, Jean, and to her parents, David and Catherine Muir

Explanatory Notes on the Text

N. B. Footnotes in the memoir *Reflections Through The Mist* (that begins on page 7) are **my** footnotes referring to my mother's story.

Short time breaks are represented by new lines; longer breaks by a large asterisk. Where a short time break occurs at the head or the foot of a page, a smaller asterisk is inserted to denote such a break.

Where Scottish characters appear, I have written Scottish dialogue in the regional accent characteristic of the area in the southern part of the county of Dumfries and Galloway (where the Muir family comes from).

A glossary of pronunciation is provided overleaf. However, it is hoped that once the reader has 'tuned in' to the accent and becomes used to it, its context will give meaning without resorting to frequent reference to the glossary.

In some instances, the accent applied to a word depends on its context and the flow of sounds in that context. For example, the reader is likely to encounter words such as hae (have), tak (take), mak (make), and iss (me or us) spoken with the English sound rather than in the local accent.

The glossary is, of course, not intended to be as comprehensive as a Scottish dictionary. Rather it aims to include most of the common words spoken by some of the principal characters.

Glossary: local Scottish accent and **dialect** into English

a'	all
a'bdy or a'body	everybody
a'reet; a'wis	alright; always
aboot	about
afore	before
ain (as in p<u>ain</u>)	own; e.g. on your own
airmy	army
Ah (as in "<u>arm</u>")	I
Ah'm; Ah'll; Ah'd; Ah've	I'm; I'll; I'd; I've
an a'	as well
auld	old
aye	expression of affirmation
alane	alone
aroon	around
awfy	awful
baith	both
bi (as in b<u>it</u>)	by (or via)
bits	boots
caal (as in c<u>a</u>r)	cold
d'ye	do you
dain	doing
dae (as in "t<u>ea</u>")	do
daes (as in "f<u>izz</u>")	does
denner	dinner
din	done
dinted	affected something
doon	down
dram	drink
duv	do
ee (as in "t<u>ee</u>") or ye	you
ee'll; ee've; ee're	you'll; you've; you're
efter	after
'em	them
f'ree	for you
fairm	farm
faither	father

fi (as in "f<u>i</u>t")	for
fin	find
fret	worry
fri	from
fun	found
gaen	gone
garn	go; going
greet; greetin	cry (tears); crying
guid	good
hae; haen (as in "h<u>ay</u>")	have; having
had (as in h<u>ar</u>d)	hold
hame	home
han	hand
hoose	house
how?	why?
intae	into
iss (as in "h<u>i</u>ss")	me or us
ken	know
kin	can
lang	long
ma (as in 'h<u>a</u>t")	my
mair	more
mak	make
masell	myself
min (as in m<u>i</u>ne)	mind; remember
(the) moran	tomorrow
(the) moran's moran	the day after tomorrow
(the) moran's night	tomorrow evening
nae (as in "Dis<u>ney</u>")	no
havenae; disnae	haven't; doesn't
wouldnae; wusnae	wouldn't; wasn't
isnae; wullnae	isn't; will not
dinnae; couldnae	don't; couldn't
cannae; didnae	can't; didn't
mustnae	mustn't
naebdie	nobody
na or nah	(also for) no

neet	night
no	not
noo (as in "wh<u>o</u>")	now
numpty	idiot
o'	of
ony; onything; onyway	any; anything; anyway
oor	our; hour
oors	ours; hours
oot	out
ower	over
piece	sandwich
pit	put
reet	right
roon	round
schuil (as in "skill")	school
sna (as in st<u>a</u>r); snaing	snow; snowing
tae (as in "t<u>i</u>p")	to
(the) day/night	today/tonight
tak	take
telt	told
thae	those
til	to
twa	two
wee	small
weel	well
weshing	washing
whee or whi	who
wheesht	be quiet
whit; whit's; whit're	what; what's; what're
wi	with
wid	wood; would
wis	was
wull	will
yer; yersel	your; yourself
yin	one
yiss	use; e.g. not much use
yissed	used (as in "used to")

Prologue

An Ending and a Beginning

My wife found it buried beneath years of accumulated domestic paperwork.

Annette was clearing out the bottom drawer of the bureau where my mother kept important documents, letters, and utility bills. I was sorting through the pile that built up around my feet.

Annette held up a slim notebook. 'I think you ought to see this,' she said after glancing at the first page.

The front cover bore a crown with the letter E to its left and an R to its right. SUPPLIED FOR THE PUBLIC SERVICE was printed just beneath the crown of Elizabeth Regina with SO BOOK 321 in a large, bold font in the centre of the cover.

'Something Mum got from work ages ago?' I suggested.

'Open it then.'

Intrigued, I turned to the first page. The heading read:

REFLECTIONS THROUGH THE MIST
INTRODUCTION

I read the first page. On it, my mother is looking back over her life on a wet, misty morning in 1974, before beginning a chapter that recalled her childhood. I turned a few pages without reading them: the notebook contained more than forty sides of writing.

I looked at Annette in disbelief. 'She's even given us a title. To think of the number of times I suggested that she should write her story. And she did it without saying a word to us. What a find!'

'She knew we'd find it.'

I wonder where it takes her up to.

'Anything else in the drawer?'

'Only her photo album.'

'Which she showed us some time ago,' I said.

'We haven't seen this either.' Annette handed me a photograph. It had been lying in the bottom of the drawer. 'Look at Jean in her wedding dress.'

It took me a while before I realised what I was looking at. I had never seen a photograph of my father. There he stood, next to my mother: a tall man in army uniform, grinning broadly. My mother and father stood at the centre of a group of twenty or so wedding guests outside an arched church door.

A lifetime of not wanting to know anything about him and here he is. What a shock.

'That's it. The bureau is empty,' said Annette. 'Let's take the important stuff home. We can shred the rest later. C'mon, you've had an emotional morning.'

Later that week Mum's flat was empty. Apart from jewellery and a few other items of sentimental value, everything else had gone to charities. We stood in Mum's living room, drawn to the pattern of indentations in the russet-coloured carpet that spoke of her modest homemaking.

The reality of my mother's possessions given away, leaving an empty space waiting for someone else to fill with their property and memories, amplified the finality of her death and deepened my grief. The empty rooms were stripped of a life, long in years and marked with struggle and ill health.

No more would I hear her call, 'Is that you, David?' when I brought her weekly shopping. No longer would I see her looking out on the garden from her armchair, barely able to read or watch television. My mother's world had shrunk in the months prior to her passing, and her body had "worn out" as she used to complain, the passing of time marked by her faculties waning one by one.

Jean was gone, but she left her story, this story.

We closed the front door, posted the keys in the letterbox of her neighbour Doris, and departed from my mother's flat for the last time.

Reflections Through The Mist

Based on and inspired by the
memoir of Jean Etheridge
1917–2013

Introduction

November 1974

As I trudged through the churchyard of Birmingham cathedral on a very wet and misty morning on my way to work, I heard myself asking:

'What is it all about?'

'Where have I been?'

'Where am I going?'

I couldn't answer the first question: does anyone know? To the second, I answered "Nowhere"; to the third "Who knows?". No, I take that back. I should know: it is up to the individual.

Perhaps it was a combination of the miserable weather, worries about my health, and living alone in a very draughty flat that prompted me to reflect on my life as I made my way past the cathedral, following the same route that I had taken many times during the war more than thirty years ago. The wartime image in my mind of the cathedral was clear and sharp; today it was shrouded in mist, as if my life too was shrouded in a fog of uncertainty.

I could not escape the weight on my mind that morning, leading me to ask what I have done with my life and could it have been any different. Questions that I had no answers to during my weary walk to work.

Chapter One

Childhood

'Run and get it, Jeanie,' shouted my sister. 'Ah'll away tae the other side.'

It was easy to see the coal in the snow. The fireman had hurled a good handful as the Glasgow train slowed to cross the bridge.

I shook the snow from our shiny black treasure and dropped it into Ma's old canvas shopping bag. Marion waved from the fence opposite.

'C'mon roon. The Cairle train's due.' [1]

We waited, listening for the singing of the rails.

'Here its,' whispered Marion. 'Get ready.'

We clung to the top of the fence with one hand, waved wildly with the other and shouted our "hellos" at the top of our lungs.

Pieces of coal flew over our heads and plopped into the snow. We didn't wait to watch the carriages rattle by.

'That's another four pieces, big yins tae,' said Marion as she blew the snow off chunks of coal and dropped them into the bag.

'Let's get some wid on oor way hame,' said my sister as we scrambled down the railway embankment.

'Why is there nae coal at hame?' I asked.

'Ah dinnae ken, Jeanie,' replied Marion. 'It's just yin o' thae things.'

---

[1] The Fechan pronunciation of Carlisle, a city just over the border with England twenty miles to the south of Ecclefechan.

I looked to my sister Marion for answers because she was older than me. I was too young to understand why we were poor, why there was often no money for coal or wood. Her answer left me walking in silence along the snow-covered lane.

'How're we tae fin wid in a' this sna?' I pleaded. 'Can't we garn hame. Ah'm caal.'

'Aye, we've got enough fri before. Let's get hame,' said Marion.

My sister held my hand as we tramped through the snow, our flimsy winter boots no protection against the wet chill of deep snow seeping into our stocking feet.

'Ma's tummy is big again,' I said.

'Aye, that's another yin on the way.'

'Where'll we a' sleep?'

'Twa tae a bed,' replied Marion.

'And if there's mair?'

'Three tae a bed.'

'Three!'

'Aye. There's only twa beds.'

We neared the village; silence filled the space left by my sister's puzzling answers.

It was almost dark as we entered the broad High Street. Oil lamps cast faint yellow shadows onto the snow, thrusting our small Scottish border village of Ecclefechan into the grip of a wintry evening.

Marion ran along the entry between Numbers 2 and 3. I trotted behind her, eager for my mother's praise at our fuel-gathering exploits.

Our house was of the one down, one up variety, typical of many in the village. Some were a little larger with two rooms upstairs. My older brother, Davie, slept in one bed, Marion and I in the other. Mother and Father slept downstairs, with my baby sister Kathy in a homemade cot. The downstairs room served as a bedroom, kitchen, and bathroom, as well as a place to eat meals cooked over an open fire. We had no electricity in those days; oil lamps were our source of light and the open fire provided heating and a means to heat water.

Day to day living revolved around the large table in the centre of the room. We washed ourselves using a basin placed on the large well-srcrubbed table, ate our meals that Mother prepared over the open fire, and sat around it during the day.[2] A midden in the backyard served as our toilet.[3]

I had become accustomed to the six of us living in our tiny, terraced house. With a brother or sister on the way, I decided for myself that a third bed would solve the sleeping problem that troubled my young mind.

Father returned from work moments after Marion and I came through the back door.

'Did ee get some coal?' he asked, draping his working clothes on the fender so that they gave off their peculiar and familiar odour as they dried, blocking the open fire.

'Aye, they did weel,' my mother answered. 'The scuttle is nearly full again.'

'Well done, lassies,' said Father. 'There's nae much work, Kate,' he said, directing his attention away from us. 'What they dae helps,' he said, smiling at us.

'Davie fun some wid an a',' said Mother. 'It's under the shelter in the yard.'

'It might be dry enough tae burn in a day or two. Hae we a stew the night, Mother?'

---

[2] Jean makes no mention of having a bath.
[3] An outdoor privy.

My mother dished out portions of vegetable stew and cut thick slices of white bread for everyone and a scone for Pa. 'There'll be meat next time. Ah'll be paid for dain the weshin' the moran.'

'Aye, grand,' said Father. 'Ah'll away on my bike the moran tae see whit work Ah can get.'

Mother swung the hook that held the cooking pot over the fire. 'There's a bit mair for ee, Davey,' she said to my father.

After our meal, Mother and Father cleared the table. Mother took the dishes into the yard to rinse them in the shared washhouse.[4] A bowl of cold water on the kitchen table provided tooth cleaning and washing for us bairns. If Mother boiled the kettle over the fire, she might take the chill off the water from the outside tap during the winter months.

'Away ee garn noo,' commanded Father.

We needed little invitation to run upstairs. My brother Davie had his own bed; Marion and I hugged each other tightly in the other bed.

'Nae caal enough fi the hot water bottle the night,' observed my sister.

'Ah've got it,' said Davie.

'That's no fair,' said Marion a little too loudly for my parents liking.

'Wheesht, up there,' Mother called out.

'Ee a'wis get it first,' added my sister in a quieter voice.

'Ah've nae yin tae cuddle up tae,' muttered Davie.

'Well, it's oor turn the moran's night,' whispered Marion.

---

[4] I've assumed this, as my mother makes no mention of washing clothes and dishes.

13

I hated the stone bed warmer after it gave up its meagre warmth. It lay immobile near the foot of the bed, cold and forgotten until one of us banged our foot on it, waking us to a cold morning.

I remember the wonderful smell of baking on Monday mornings, an aroma that urged us to leave our cold beds and dash downstairs.

Mother would always be the first to rise, light the fire and prepare breakfast for Father before he cycled to work or to find work; he would be gone by the time the kitchen aromas drifted upstairs.

A small oven formed part of the large open fire arrangement. Mother made fruit tarts, loaves, and cakes. Tattie scones and drop scones were made on the open fire on a girdle, which hung from one of the hooks that could be swung over the fire.[5]

My father didn't care for bread; he much preferred scones that Mother made regularly. Thinking about it now, I wonder if his dislike of bread had anything to do with his experience as a prisoner of war.[6]

At that age, I didn't understand why we sometimes went hungry, or why the oven wasn't used for a week or two. I just thought that it was normal to have something to eat one day and very little the next.

When Father did find work, eggs, milk, and butter could be bought from the village farm nearby.

Marion and Davie were the first to be given breakfast before they left for school in the village.

---

[5] Girdle is the local term for a griddle pan, used to make scones.
[6] Please see *There Was A Soldier*.

14

'It'll be your turn tae garn next year, Jeanie,' Mother would say to me when there were just the two of us left downstairs.

'Ah want tae stay here with you, Ma,' I would wail. 'Ah dinnae want tae garn.'

'Dinnae be daft. Ee've got tae garn tae the schuil. Ee've got tae learn.'

'Ah can learn fri you, Ma,' I insisted.

Mother shrugged and sighed. 'C'mon, help me wi the cleaning.'

The fire grate was kept highly polished with black lead, a liquid that was applied with a rag, left to dry then buffed to a mirror shine. A fender kept us children away from the open fire. All the steel and brass parts of the fender and the fire tools were polished once a week using emery paper.

'Sit yersel doon and polish the poker and a',' insisted Mother.

I didn't like this job, but at least I could sit at one end of the fender bench and feel the warmth of the fire.

The bench had a padded box at either end. Fire cleaning and shoe cleaning things were kept in one end, kindling wood in the other.

On winter days I would sit on one of the boxes and do my cleaning duties. When my brother and sister came in from school, there would be fights over who sat near the fire on the other end of the bench.

On summer days, we kept away from the fire. It still had to be lit so that my mother could cook meals and bake.

In the summer before my sixth birthday, prior to going to school, I started work on the village farm. From the eldest to the youngest, we worked on the farm until we left school, earning much-needed income to help support the family. The girls in our family helped with cleaning cowsheds and hen houses, washing out milk churns and scrubbing the milking parlour.

One of my jobs was in the farm's smithy, where I operated the bellows. I can almost hear the hammer on the anvil as I write this part of my memoir: it made a delightful ringing tone.

My other jobs included helping the farmer's wife make butter every morning after the other girls had finished their chores and left for school.

'Ah'll hae tae fin a new assistant soon, Jeanie,' said Mrs MacMurray. 'Ee'll be off tae the schuil next week.'

'Can Ah still come and help oot efter schuil?'

'Aye, ee can. Ah'll fin ee a wee job until ee're auld enough fi the milk round. Here's a bit extra the day.'

'A shilling!' exclaimed Mother when I handed over my wages.

'Can Ah still work efter schuil?' I asked.

'Ee'll hae tae, Jeanine. The family's growing.'

Mother's stomach was growing again: number five was on the way.

Chapter Two

School Days and Holidays

'Had ma han, Jeanie,' said Marion as we walked along the High Street on our way to my first day at school.

My sister, three years older than me, took me to a room, knocked and led me in.

'Ah, hello, Jean,' said the teacher, a very tall woman dressed entirely in grey, with her white hair pulled back into a tight bun. 'There's a spare desk,' she said, pointing at the front row.

'Are ee no stayin'?' I asked my sister.

'Nah. Ah'm in the older class,' she replied to a restrained chorus of tittering. 'Ah'll see ee later.'

I faintly remember starting school with several other girls. I hid my ignorance about what I was supposed to do and took comfort in the shared shyness of the other new girls.

The older girls in my class kept themselves to themselves to begin with, as though they felt it beneath them to make friends with us new ones. After a few days though, we were accepted as if we had been at school before the summer holidays.

I earned the respect of my classmates by being good at netball and rounders. I enjoyed subjects that required me to sit at my desk, writing on slates, but I longed to be outside taking part in sport.

I must have been about ten or eleven years of age when Mother and Mrs MacMurray agreed that I could start work delivering milk around the village before and after school, a task that was particularly arduous on cold winter mornings and dark winter evenings.

At the end of my first day, my shoulders ached from carrying wooden pails of milk suspended from a yoke across my shoulders.

'Ee'll get yissed tae it,' claimed Mother.

'At least they get lighter towards the end of the roon,' I said.

I handed all my wage of two shillings and sixpence to Mother at the end of my first week and every week after that.[7]

To make extra money for Mother, I cleaned shoes for the farmer's son: tuppence a pair.

I also called upon an elderly lady after I finished delivering the milk in the morning and after school to run errands for her. She gave me a half-penny on weekdays and a penny on Saturdays. She often gave me a piece (a sandwich), for which I was always grateful.

These were times of hunger. There was often no work for Father, no money coming in apart from what us children earned, and little or no food to feed our growing family. Many is the time that we stole fruit from orchards and swedes and turnips from nearby fields. We would skin and eat them straight out of the ground when we felt very hungry, making our bellies ache.

Father gathered potatoes on Saturdays when he had no other work. It was my job to follow him along the furrows, knock the soil off the potatoes before putting them in a basket. My reward from Father was tuppence

---

[7] Twelve and a half pence in today's Sterling currency.

or sixpence, pocket money that I was allowed to keep to spend on the annual Sunday School outing to the seaside or at the yearly village fair.

Early childhood memories are fleeting. It never occurred to me that we might move to a larger house or that we could have more food. I simply thought that is how it was for most families in the village. Being cold and hungry are things that I got used to.

Such feelings almost erase memories of long warm summer holidays from school, happy times wandering the countryside surrounding our village, exploring freedom in the open air, away from the confines of our crowded house.

Marion and I roamed the nearby glens, gathering wild flowers to take home to Mother. We collected shivering grasses and wild strawberries from the railway banks and grass verges of the country lanes.

'Ah'll wesh them fi oor tea,' Mother would say. 'Some folks hae strawberries a' the time. That's how the other half live.'

I always wondered who this other half were every time I heard my mother say it. My experience of these mysterious people came to me when I finished my first year in the senior school.

I set off for the farm on the first day of the summer holidays. The morning dawned clear, promising a warm day.

'A new customer for ee the day, Jean,' said Mrs MacMurray. 'There's guests at The Hall.'

I knocked on the back door of the large house on the edge of the village. A smartly dressed woman came to the door with her jug at the ready.

'Do you deliver every day?' she asked in a posh voice.

'Morning and evening,' I replied.

Later in the week, a girl of about my age answered the door.

'Hello, I'm Sheila,' she said, dipping a jug into one of my milk pails.

'Ah'm Jean. Ah've not seen ee in the village afore.'

'We're here for the holidays. This is my grandparents' house,' she replied.

I could see past her into a large room, much larger than ours.

'I don't know anyone in Ecclefechan. My sisters are much older than me.'

My eyes were suddenly diverted to something on the floor just inside the door. Sheila followed my gaze.

'Oh, my roller skates. I must put them away. Mother will be cross.'

I continued to stare.

'Have you never … would you like a go on them?'

I could only manage a vigorous nod. 'Efter my roon,' I said excitedly. 'Can Ah call later?'

What fun I had bowling along the Glasgow to Carlisle Road that skirted the village, dodging the traffic.

The friendship between Sheila and me lasted every summer until I left school. How happy I felt being singled out to be her friend. After all, Sheila and her sisters were obviously much better educated than me, went to a posh school, were much better dressed than me and were well-spoken with English accents. I shall never know why she singled me out as a friend. Perhaps the other half didn't look down on my half.

I looked up to them, or at least to Sheila's grandparents: their house was very large.

I had never seen a bathroom or a separate kitchen before. Neither had I ever seen an inside toilet: a flush one at that. The Hall was a house beyond my dreams, one that I never thought I would venture inside.

Sheila's mother looked out clothes for me before her family left The Hall at the end of the summer holidays, items that the family didn't need any longer. These clothes were in very good condition. Mother was always very grateful for them, as there was never very much by way of new clothes for us children, only hand-me-downs.

The end of my final year at senior school saw the end of my friendship with Sheila. The family left their grandparents' house at the end of the summer holidays in 1931. It is conceivable that Sheila, like me, reached the age of 14 and left school.

Perhaps friendship is as fleeting as childhood memories: I never saw Sheila again.

Chapter Three

Leaving School

My school certificate, dated 3rd October 1931, denoted that my Character and Conduct was 'VG', as was English, History, and Geography. Maths, Arithmetic, and Science merited a 'G'. Cookery, Laundry, Housewifery, and Needlework also scored 'VG'.

Perhaps my reported practical housekeeping skills propelled me towards employment as a housekeeper. Mother and Father certainly thought so.

Whilst early childhood memories often vanish quickly, harsher times trigger bleaker, longer-lasting memories.

As soon as each of us children left school, we were sent out to work. We were a poor family; earning a wage to help keep the family had to be done. I was the third of eight children when I left home in 1931, shortly after my fourteenth birthday.

My elder sister Marion and elder brother Davie had already left, leaving Mother, Father, and five younger siblings in our over-crowded home.

I had been allowed inside Sheila's grandparents' house. I wondered if I would ever live in such grand surroundings.

*

Mother called me in the day after I left school; I was hanging washing in the back yard. 'Yer faither and me hae been talking aboot whit we should dae wi ee.'

'Aye, Ma. Whit aboot me?'

'Ee'll hae tae follow Marion and Davie and garn tae work.'

'Ah ken that much, Ma.'

'Away fri hame, Ah mean.'

'Away! How?'

'There's barely any room for iss a'.'

'We can a' fit upstairs.'

'There'll soon be another mouth tae feed. We need mair money coming in.'

Ah thought as much.

'Where'll Ah garn?'

'Yer faither kens some people over Dalton way. They need help on their smallholding.'

'Is there nae work in the Fechan?'

'There's nothing, Jeanie. There's been hardly any work since the end of the war. Faither struggles every day tae fin work. We desperately need ee tae work fi the family.'

I had no say in the matter; that much was obvious.

A few days later, I packed my few clothes in a carpet bag of mother's and set off for the two-hour walk to Dalton, a small village to the west of Ecclefechan.

From this distance, I can't remember the names of the elderly couple I worked for. They were pleasant enough, but they made me work very hard inside their house and outside on the smallholding.

This was an unhappy time for me, living away from home, miles from anywhere, working long hours for poor pay. I was allowed to go home for one half day a week: a Sunday afternoon. By the time I walked home, it was almost time to start the long walk back in time to prepare the tea.

I lasted about a year at the smallholding, until the elderly woman fell seriously ill and was taken to hospital in Dumfries. Her husband put the house and farm up for sale. I can't remember what happened to the couple after I left.

I stayed at my Aunty Chrissie's before my next job came along. Our house was far too crowded, even after moving along the street to a one-down, two-up. My aunty lived on her own, so there was room for me.

'Lucky for ee, ma lodger is away,' she said when I arrived from Dalton for the last time.

'Thanks, Aunty. Oor hoose is awfy crowded the noo.'

'Aye, well. Ah'm beginning tae lose count o' ma nephews and nieces.'

'Ah'm the third of nine,' I reminded her.

My aunty shrugged, glanced at me and shook her head. 'Mair tea?'

'Aye, please.'

'It's the Mop in the moran's moran,' said my aunty.[8]

'Aye, Ah ken. Ah'm in it.'

My aunty shook her head again, muttering while she refilled the teapot.

'Ah dinnae approve, Jeanie. It's nae a proper way o' dain things.'

'It's a'wis been the way,' I suggested.

'Disnae mak it reet,' she snapped. 'Sorry, Jeanie. Just be careful. Whitever happens, tak care o' yersel.'

---

[8] A hiring fair.

*

I can still see myself standing glum and silent with boys and girls lined up with me in the High Street outside our house while farmers and their wives walked up and down the line until they made their choice.

A red-faced farmer stopped and pointed at me for a second time. 'Aye, she'll dae. Where're yer people, lassie?'

I pointed out Mother and Father.

'Garn an' wait by that horse and cart,' commanded the farmer.

The man spoke to my parents while I stood next to the cart.

'Away in and collect yer things,' he said as he strode over to where I stood. 'We'll away in an oor.'

The man joined a group of farmers on their way into the hotel. The hiring fair was at an end.

I crossed the road and collected my carpet bag from Aunty Chrissie's house. She had washed and ironed my clothes.

'Thank ee fi dain ma laundry, Aunty,' I said.

'It's nae bother, lassie. Are ee away the day?'

'Aye. Ma new boss is in the pub.'

'Aye, they're a' in there. Feelin' pleased wi themselves, Ah'll be bound. Slave labour, that's whit it is, slave labour.' Aunty Chrissie gave me a hug. 'Have ee said goodbye tae yer ma and pa?'

'No yet. Ah'm nae feeling like talking tae 'em. The whole thing wis awfy. Ah cannae pit intae words whit Ah'm feelin'. Ah've nae felt it afore. It's like a sickness in ma belly.'

'Aye, Ah ken. Ah'll speak tae 'em. Off ee garn noo. And remember, watch oot fi yersel. And the lads, min the lads.'

I returned to the street and waited for my new boss. Several carts lined the wide High Street near the Ecclefechan Hotel, each accompanied by a familiar face waiting to be taken to goodness knows where and heaven knows for how long.

I didn't know what my aunty meant.

After a long wait by his cart, the farmer and his wife emerged from the hotel.

'Get yersel in the back,' the man said, his beery breath wafting into my face. I sat on a smelly sack in the back of the cart; the farmer and his wife took the box seat. I watched the High Street receding as I sat with my legs dangling.

I remember the journey to this day. I can still see the countryside falling away from me as I was taken from home by an unseen force. Compared to being sent to work for the elderly couple, I felt resentment that my parents had sold me at the Hiring Fair.

I didn't look over my shoulder at the farmer and his wife. I didn't even know if they bothered to look behind to make sure I was still there. Several times during the long journey, I thought about grabbing my carpet bag, dropping to the ground, and hiding until the cart was out of sight.

The anger at my mother and father stayed my urge to run home. It was my duty to earn for the growing family, just as Marion and Davie were doing.

After a journey that felt like hours, we arrived at a sprawling farm beyond Annan, near a village called Powfoot. I could see the sea from the farmyard, a sight that lightened my embittered spirits.

'C'mon, lassie. Ah'll show ee where ee're stayin',' said the farmer's wife.

My accommodation was no more than a converted barn. I sat on the rudimentary bed feeling very sorry for myself.

'Ye ken how tae milk coos?' snapped the farmer's wife.

'Aye,' I replied.

'That's yer first job in the moran.'

∗

Living on the farm was another unhappy period of my life. I was expected to work very hard, rising at five thirty every morning to milk the cows before returning to the farmhouse kitchen to help prepare breakfast for the farmer, his wife, and their two sons, one an adult, and the other about my age.

I never knew how the two boys put up with their father: he was a cruel man, always shouting at everyone, including his wife. I tried to make sure that I wasn't the target of a tongue-lashing by working hard and doing everything asked of me. I did not like him.

Self-protection came at a cost: life on the farm was very hard. Cleaning, scrubbing, polishing, working on the land, and being at the beck and call of everyone at all the hours that God sends seemed relentless.

I earned three pounds ten shillings per half year,[9] all of which I handed over to Mother when I went home.

There was no bus route, and it was too far to walk home. Consequently, I was taken to Ecclefechan twice a year either by my boss or by a local farmer.

---

[9] £3.50 in today's Sterling currency.

27

Escape from the drudgery of slaving for the family presented itself unexpectedly one evening during milking just over a year after the Hiring Fair: the youngest son tried to put his hand up my skirt.

The shock froze me rigid for a moment. Now I knew what my aunty meant.

I kicked the boy on the shin as hard as I could, backed away and kicked him with all my might between his legs.

He doubled up, moaning and gasping and stumbled out of the milking parlour.

I was milking the last of the cows when the boy's father burst in, holding the boy by his ear.

'Ee kicked him!' he shouted.

'He pit his han up ma skirt,' I protested.

'Ah didnae,' whimpered the boy.

'He did so,' I said. 'He's lyin'.'

The farmer dragged the boy to the door of the parlour and shoved him into the yard.

'Ah want ee gaen,' he scowled at me.

'And Ah'll be telling ma faither whit happened,' I replied.

The farmer muttered something and stormed out. That was my last milking on his farm.

I packed my carpet bag at first light the following morning and walked to Annan to find the road to Ecclefechan. I went directly to Aunty Chrissie's house.

'Whit're ee dain here, Jeannie?' she said when she opened her front door.

'Can Ah stay here please?'

'Aye, of course. Ah've nae lodger. Whit's happened? Ah can see that ee're upset.'

I told my aunty of the events of the past day or two.

'Where did ee kick him?'

'In the balls.'

'Well done. Good for ee. He deserved it.'

'Whit dae Ah tell Ma and Pa?'

'The truth, Jean. Wait till the moran though. Ee dinnae need tae garn hame the night.'

'He owes iss fi the past few weeks,' I told my mother the next morning. 'Ah'm nae garn back there. Ah'll fin ma ain job this time.

My mother took my word for the reason for my departure from the farm. Father was angry, even when I told him what I had told my mother. I was determined that I would have a say in the matter from now on.

*

It turned out that I didn't have a say in the matter of my next job. At the age of 17, work took me away from home again, this time to be employed as a maid to a retired doctor and his wife. They lived in Carlisle just over the English border, about 20 miles from Ecclefechan. The doctor's wife was a very rigid, unfriendly woman. Mrs Robertson always addressed me by my surname: Muir.

Once again, this was not a happy time in my young life. I had to rise early and work hard on domestic duties and chores throughout the day, as well as wait at table for the doctor and his wife every day and when they held dinner parties and cocktail evenings.

I had one half day off per week as well as every other Sunday when I took the bus home for the day.

I can't remember how much I was paid. I managed to persuade my parents to let me keep some of my wages. I clearly remember buying my first coat with my own money. It was emerald green with silver buttons in a fashionable military style.

I needed my own money to buy clothes so that I looked smartly dressed and presentable, even though my maid's uniform came with the job. My uniform consisted of a long print dress, covered by a white apron complete with a bib for morning wear. Afternoon wear was a long alpaca dress, which reached almost to the floor, over which I wore a starched apron that had an embroidered edge with long flowing strings carefully tied in a neat bow. In addition, I wore a white cap: one for mornings and a differently styled one for the afternoons and evenings.

Although the hours were long, the regime strict and unforgiving, at least I worked indoors. I soon learnt how to fulfil my role: I was good at domestic tasks; I became a good maid and housekeeper.

The doctor and his wife treated me well, although rather strict in their demands. Perhaps previous maids had not come up to the mark.

I never needed telling twice. I knew that I was good at my job, but I hid the constant feeling of dissatisfaction that lurked within me: would I always be destined to be someone's servant or housekeeper; was this the sole fulfilment of the prediction of my school certificate?

Now that I recall my teenage years and beyond, I spent most of the 1930s employed in a variety of domestic jobs, working away from home for poor pay, nearly all of which was handed over to my parents.

My childhood and adulthood were characterised by poverty at home and hardship at work in the years following the First World War. These are what some people call "the good old days". Not a bit of it: slave labour is what I call it. Upstairs and downstairs with no in-between.

What happened next turned my life upside down.

Chapter Four

Call Up

'Madam, may I have some time off this afternoon?' I asked when I set the coffee tray down.

'And why would that be, Muir?' said Mrs Robertson sternly.

Doctor Robertson lowered his newspaper and joined his wife in glaring at me as if I had asked for a pay rise.

'I have to register for war work this afternoon at the Labour Exchange.'

'Really, how do you know?' he demanded.

'It was in yesterday's paper, sir. You said that I could read the papers when you have finished with them.'

'Why you, now? Today?'

'It is the turn of twenty to twenty-five-year-olds. I must register. It is my duty to do so.'

The doctor and his wife exchanged a glance before resuming their contemplation of me in their usual superior manner.

'And what about us, Muir?' exclaimed Mrs Robertson.

'I expect that I will be sent away to do some sort of work for the war effort, madam. All single women are being called up. I have to report at two o'clock. I don't know how long it will take to register, but I will return as soon as possible.'

'Very well,' said Mrs Robertson. 'We have been half-expecting something like this. We have no choice in the matter. Your duty will soon no longer be with us. It will be elsewhere. You may take the afternoon off.'

'Thank you, sir, madam. I will come straight back. Have you finished?'

'Yes, please clear away,' said Mrs Robertson, with a perfunctory wave of her hand.

I gathered up the coffee things and carried the tray into the kitchen, hoping that I wouldn't have to fetch and carry for the doctor and his wife for very much longer.

The first 18 months of the war largely passed me by until that Monday in April 1941 when I learnt that my turn had come to register: the reality of contributing to the war effort was forced upon me. My older sister, Marion, ran the village post office during the war and my older brother, Davie, was in the merchant navy. As the third oldest, I was next in line to register.

I felt exhilarated as I joined a long line of women waiting outside the Labour Exchange in Carlisle that afternoon, excited to be given the opportunity to serve, to do something useful for the country. Excitement soon became tinged with anxiety as the queue reached the entrance. What would I be expected to do? Where would I be sent? These and a myriad of other questions tumbled about in my head.

It's the same for all of us, I thought, as I glanced at the worried faces behind me waiting on the pavement.

'I see that you prefer factory work to farm work', said the elderly official as he read my form.

'Yes, sir.'

'No need to "sir" me, Miss Muir,' he said with a broad smile. 'You have experience with farm work though.'

'Yes, but I thought I would like to do something different for the war.'

'Good. We need factory workers more than we need farm workers at the moment. Are you happy to proceed?'

'Yes, though I don't know what it entails.'

'All in good time. Everything will be explained when you start work.'

'When will that be? I have to give notice.'

'These arrangements take precedence. How much notice are you expected to give?'

'A month.'

'You will be required to start early in May, less than a month from now. Details will be sent to the address you've given. You'll be informed about your accommodation and so forth. You should hear in a few days. Show the letter to your employer. They will be instructed to let you go without serving out your full notice.'

My interviewer leant back in his chair, looked at me rather than at the paperwork on the desk in front of him and smiled broadly again.

'Any further questions, Miss Muir?'

'Do you know where I'll be going?'

'Birmingham, to work in a factory that makes aircraft parts. You'll be making a significant contribution to the war effort.'

I nodded as if I understood the enormity of what he told me.

The official pushed back his chair and extended his left hand. 'Well done, Miss Muir. Your contribution to the war effort will be much appreciated. Good luck.'

I thanked him, turned and made space for the next woman in the short queue behind me. We exchanged nervous glances before she took her place at the table.

The large clock over the double doors to the inner office of tables and lines of women showed me that the whole process had taken under an hour. I would be back in time to serve the doctor and his wife their afternoon tea.

Not for much longer.

For the first time in my life I felt valued other than as a skivvy; being treated with respect and politeness was a new experience. Very few adults had shaken me by the hand and addressed me as Miss Muir. I walked back to the doctor's house feeling very grown-up.

A large brown envelope addressed to me awaited my attention after breakfast on Friday 25th April. After I washed up the breakfast things, I made myself a cup of tea and spread the contents of the envelope on the kitchen table.

I was instructed to report to my new employer on Monday 5th May at nine o'clock, just over a week away. An enclosing letter released me from my present employer with immediate effect.

I could leave today.

There was also information concerning accommodation, a form to send back, as well as a booklet about factory safety and another booklet about security and secrecy.

I put everything back in the envelope, intending to read it all again later that day. I left the envelope on my bedside table, took out the letter, went downstairs and knocked on the door of the library.

The doctor read the letter, nodding slowly, murmuring occasionally. He read it for a second time before handing it back to me.

'Well, Muir, when do you intend to leave?'

'In the morning, sir.'

'Why wait? The Ministry has given you permission to leave our employ immediately.'

'What will you do about your meals today?'

'That is no concern of yours any longer. You need time at home to prepare to do your duty. I'm too old, of course. I did my bit in the first war.'

'So did my father, sir.'

'You don't need to work out your last day. My wife is visiting her sister. I'll explain what is happening when she returns after lunch. Please look in when you are ready to leave.'

It didn't take me long to pack my few clothes in my mother's worn-out carpet bag. I left the bag in the hall and knocked on the door of the library for the second time that morning.

'I hope that you don't think harshly of us, Muir,' said Doctor Robertson. 'The fact that you have stayed with us for, what, six years is it? You're the best housekeeper we've ever had.'

They didn't show it much.

'After the war, if you need a reference let us know.'

'Thank you, sir.'

'There's a little extra here,' said the doctor, handing me an envelope.

'Thank you, sir.'

'Goodbye, Muir. And good luck.'

At least I didn't have to explain myself to her.

I closed the library door, put my wages in my handbag, picked up the carpet bag and left the house without looking back. I forgot to tell the doctor that I'd left my outfits neatly ironed and laid out on my bed.

Aunty Chrissie was surprised when I landed on her front doorstep that afternoon.

'It's Friday, whit're ee dain hame?'

I explained over a cup of tea.

'Can Ah stay here until Ah'm away?'

'Of course. Ee ken this is yer hame. There'll just be yersel and Danny in the small bedroom.[10] Kathy is away at her work in Dumfries.

My four younger brothers and sister Betty took up what little space there was at Ma and Pa's house further along the High Street.

'Thanks, Aunty. It's still too crowded at home. Do you think Murray will be the last?'

'Aye, Ah reckon so. Almost lost yer accent then.'

'Six years amongst the English, Aunty. Not much Scottish spoken in Carlisle.'

'When d'ye hae tae be in Birmingham of a' places? God, that's ower twa hunnerd miles doon there in England.'

'I start war work in a factory a week on Monday. I'll catch a train next Saturday so that I can get settled intae ma digs.'

---

[10] My aunty has always been known as "Danny"; she was christened Diana.

'Aye well, Jean. Kathy and Danny likely wull be next. Everyone'll be away dain something fi the war. It disnae seem five minutes since that last yin.'

'Never mind, Aunty. We'll a' be hame one day.'

Aunty Chrissie cleared away cups and saucers, muttering to herself.

'Ah'm away up the street, Aunty.'

'We're proud of ee, Jean,' said my father.

'Aye, that we are,' rejoined my mother.

'Parts fi planes,' commented my father.

'That's all Ah know,' I replied. 'Ah daresay Ah'll fin oot more soon enough.'

'Wull ee get ony leave?'

'That Ah don't know, Ma. Ah'll write as soon as Ah know.'

The solemnity of the moment was broken when five children clattered into the room.

'Ah'll leave ee tae it, Ma.'

William, Betty, Angus, Hiddleston, and Murray barely paid me any heed as they flung their school bags down. The boys hurtled upstairs and Betty offered to help Ma get their tea ready.

Father came to the door and out onto the street with me. 'When d'ye leave?'

'Ah've tae be at work on Monday, so Ah'll catch a train on Saturday.

Father's kind blue-grey eyes revealed his sadness and he looked at me wordlessly.

'Ah'll be fine, Pa,' I said, in an attempt to reassure him.

Father sighed his face brightened a little. 'Aye, well take care o' yersel.'

'You too. You've got all the bairns to look after. Us older yins can look efter oorselves.'

Father looked away through the open front door, then back at me, his face serious again. 'The big cities are being bombed, Jean. Ye'll need tae watch oot for yersel. It'll no be like Carlisle.'

'Aye, Ah know, Pa. Dinnae fret,' I said, patting his arm.

'Ee havenae completely lost yer accent then?'

'Almost. Working for the folk in Carlisle has dinted it.'

'Ah'll away in. See iss afore ee leave.'

'Of course.'

I watched Father go in and close the front door. I think he wanted to tell me something, but whatever it was he held back.

The wartime railway timetables were subject to last-minute alterations according to Father. Nevertheless, the timetable on the notice board in the Post Office showed that there was a train on Saturday 3rd May at 11:55 from Carlisle to Birmingham.

Aunty Chrissie lent me a suitcase. 'That auld carpet bag o' yer Ma's is din. Ee'll need a proper case.'

Friday evening came: the evening of my big adventure. I had never been on a train; I had never been further away from home than Carlisle. All I could do was to imagine that Birmingham would be a larger version of the city where I had lived and worked for the past few years.

A small crowd lingered at the bus stop in the High Street, waiting with me for the Lockerbie to Carlisle bus. As soon as we saw it turn off the main road, hugs and tear-choked "goodbyes" began.

Danny and Chrissie wiped their cheeks while Ma gave me a fierce hug. Pa got on the bus with my suitcase, said something to the driver and stepped onto the pavement to let me on. He held me for a long time, neither of us able to say anything.

At length, he let me go.

'Goodbye, Jeanie,' he whispered, then he walked to the back of the crowd. I couldn't see his face, but I had felt his sadness in his quivering embrace and heard it in his voice.

I held on to my tears until the bus drew away, leaving my family waving and calling my name, barely audible over the rattle of the bus and the shudder of its ancient engine.

I had left home on the Carlisle bus on many occasions: this time felt different, more significant and vital. Instead of the resignation of returning to the doctor's large house to be of service to him and his strict wife, I felt a potent mixture of excitement and trepidation.

The notion of working in a factory in a large city two hundred miles away from home was utterly alien to me. I could not even begin to imagine what the next chapter in my life would be like.

I put the doubts and fears to the back of my mind and stared out of the window, wondering when next I would see my family.

The railway station at Carlisle bustled with weekend travellers, a good proportion of them made up by men in khaki, laughing and back-slapping in groups here and there in the concourse and on the platforms.

There seemed to be soldiers everywhere, their camaraderie evident in their loud voices and pride in their appearance. Any unaccompanied woman was met with sparkling smiles and a touch of a cap or beret.

One group that I approached as I made my way along my platform stopped talking, smiled to a man and touched their caps almost in unison as I passed by. They would not have seen me redden, but I could hear what I took to be respectful calls of "hello, miss" aimed by two or three of them in my direction, followed by "sit with us, love", a request that seemed less respectful and rather intimidating.

I worried that I would be the only woman in a compartment of soldiers all the way to Birmingham.

I chose a compartment with no soldiers and one unaccompanied seat next to the corridor. An elderly man put my case up onto the luggage rack and was almost knocked off his feet as the train jerked into life. Hands went out to stop him landing in someone's lap.

'Thank you,' I said when he took his seat.

'My pleasure, miss', he replied. 'Going far?'

'Birmingham.'

'A long way.'

'The furthest I will be from home in my whole life and this is my first time on a train.'

These admissions caused a buzz of comments and questions amongst my fellow passengers. I did my best to answer everyone.

'Good for you, dear,' said the elderly man's wife. 'We need youngsters to take up the men's work.'

*

I dozed off and on during the long journey south. By the time we drew into the station at Birmingham, only the mother and her young son remained from Carlisle: three soldiers sat opposite, grinning at me.

One of them took my case down. 'Here you are, love,' he said, his breath an unpleasant mixture of beer and cigarettes.

'Thank you,' I replied, eager to escape the crowded compartment.

'Good luck,' said the boy's mother.

'Aye, thanks,' I replied.

I joined the line of people in the corridor moving slowly towards the exit door of the carriage. Cigarette smoke and the odour of sweaty bodies almost overwhelmed me as I shuffled along, desperate for fresher air.

I stepped onto the platform, gasping and struggling to pull my case out of the carriage door quickly enough to let passengers out who were behind me. The crowded platform offered no fresh air. Smoke, steam and the noise of hundreds of people rushing in all directions froze me to the spot. I was bumped into several times as I looked about me.

'Don't stand there,' snapped a tall man as he shoved past me, almost knocking me over.

I guessed the direction to the exit and moved towards it, drawn into a throng of hurrying humanity until I spotted an exit sign pointing up a flight of steps. The crowd surged upwards, carrying me with it into a spacious concourse, much larger than the entrance to Carlisle station. I aimed for the side nearest to me and flopped onto a wooden bench, placing my case at my feet. Getting off the train had been an ordeal.

Is it always like this here?

I sat for a few minutes, mesmerised by the tide of people, their toing and froing presumably hiding some purpose and activity.

My next task was to find the correct bus to Smethwick. My envelope of instructions included an address in what I took to be a part of Birmingham. I looked about the edges of the concourse for an information window.

Eventually I found somewhere that looked like it might provide advice. I waited in a short queue until I reached the front.

'Yes,' barked the man behind the window.

'Can you tell me which bus—'

'This is train enquiries,' he snapped.

'Where might bus enquiries be?' I pleaded.

'Not here. Move along please.'

I picked up my case and moved aside.

Now what?

The smoke from what seemed like dozens of steam engines filled the concourse with acrid air that stung my throat. I decided to find my way out of the station.

There was no let-up in the crowds immediately beyond the exit; Carlisle was placid by comparison.

Rows of taxis lined both sides of the street. There were no buses to be seen. I had hoped to ask the first conductor I came across. I could see a street leading up a short hill away from the station and set off through the crowds of Saturday afternoon shoppers.

Buses; thank goodness.

I walked along the line of parked buses until I found a conductor standing on the footplate of one of them. 'You want a seventy-five, love.'

'Where from?'

'Colmore Row,' she called out as her bus pulled out into the street, busy with buses, lorries, and vans of all descriptions. My first experience of a big city left me reeling and bewildered.

Now to find this row place.

I continued up the hill until I reached a crossroads.

Which way to go?

Jostled by passers-by, I stood in a state of shock at what I saw along the street to the right. Most of the buildings were damaged, their shattered fronts lay in heaps of rubble in the road. Huge timbers settled at awkward angles amongst piles of bricks and broken glass.

These must have been shops.

Nothing had prepared me for the sight of a bombed-out street. Newspaper reports at home were vague; no pictures were published, and towns and cities that were bombed were not named. The reality of what had seemed like a distant war lay yards from where I stood.

This was real.

People would have been killed.

Livelihoods destroyed.

Here I was, a lass from the rural border with Scotland transported into the aftermath of an inferno.

I walked slowly up the hill away from the crossroads, looking for someone to ask.

'Excuse me,' I said to a young mother pushing a large pram. 'Could you tell me how I get to Colmore Row?'

'Up to the top, turn left and cross the cathedral churchyard.'

'Thank you,' I replied.

'You alright, love?'

'Yes, thank you. I've just had a shock. All that damage down there.'

'There was a massive raid a couple of weeks ago. You're not from around here then.'

'I'm just arrived from Scotland. I start war work on Monday.'

'Good on yer. Take care, love. Watch out for yourself. We're in for more raids, I reckon.'

I found the cathedral and after another enquiry with a bus conductor, I waited at the stop for the Number 75 bus. I had only a few minutes to wait.

'I'll let you know when you're in the High Street, miss. You can ask from there,' said the conductor.

The journey through the streets of Birmingham did nothing to lessen the shock of seeing the extensive bomb damage in the city centre.

At least the cathedral was spared.

I looked out of the window as the bus left the city centre behind, expecting to see more buildings without fronts, relieved to see that most houses and shops were in one piece.

Perhaps the outskirts don't get bombed so much?

Opposite one of the bus stops along a wide road, the inside of an office above a boarded-up shop front faced the street, desks and filing cabinets in full view. It looked like a giant doll's house with its front open.

That answers my question then.

I felt as if I was the only person on the bus to take any notice. Even passing pedestrians didn't bother to look up at the still intact notice board.

They must be used to all this.

The scene across the road looked even more incongruous on a sunny day. I half-expected war to take place beneath dreary skies.

'Smethwick High Street, love,' called the conductress. 'You could try asking at the library, just along there.'

'Thanks for your help,' I said as I alighted, in the hope that I wouldn't have to carry my suitcase very far to my digs.

It had been a long journey from Scotland. I wondered if the library would be open this late on a Saturday afternoon.

'Sorry to bother you,' I said to an elderly man in uniform who was standing just inside the open double doors of the library. 'Where might I get directions?'

'Where to, madam?'

'Church Road.'

'That's easy,' he said as he stepped onto the pavement and pointed. 'You go down there, to the Council House. You can't miss it. Take the left fork and it's what, second right. That's Church Road.'

I thanked the doorman and set off on what I hoped would be the last leg of my long journey from Ecclefechan, from my tiny village that felt like the other end of the world, where the war left no mark.

The faces of Ma, Pa, and Aunty Chrissie formed in my mind; pictures of Ecclefechan High Street floated before my eyes as I walked along Smethwick High Street, its share of bomb damage all too clear.

When will I see home again?

Church Road sloped sufficiently to offset the front doors of the long terrace. I walked downhill in search of Number 92.

A middle-aged woman wearing a flowing pinafore apron opened the front door.

'Yes.'

'Mrs Ellsworth?' I asked.

'Ah, you must be Miss Moor,' she said, opening the door wider.

'It's Muir,' I said. 'Not an easy one to pronounce. "Mewer", like a cat.'

'I've been expecting you. Come this way.'

I followed the person who I assumed would be my landlady along a passage.

'You can leave your case there. I'll show you your room later.'

I left my case on the floor, near the foot of the stairs. The whole length of the passage was laid with red and white diamond-shaped tiles and led to a kitchen situated at the rear of the terraced house.

Larger than the terraces in the Fechan.

'Please take a seat. Tea?'

'Oh, yes please. It's been a very long journey. I haven't had anything since I left home.'

'And where exactly is Ecclefechan, Miss Mewer?'

'Just across the border in Scotland.'

'Thank you for your letter. The Labour asked me if I would take a woman war worker. So here we are. Milk and sugar?'

'Just a splash of milk please. I imagine it's rationed?'

'Milk's not too bad. It's other things.'

'Of course,' I said. 'My home village has a farm that supplies the village with milk and dairy. I used to deliver the milk when I was younger.'

'And recently, your job I mean?'

'Housekeeper for a retired doctor and his wife.'

'This is going to be a lot different, factory work I mean.'

'Well, yes. I've done a lot of farm work before housekeeping, so I chose factory work instead. It's going to take some getting used to.'

My landlady took several sips of her tea, as if to give herself some thinking time.

'I live here on my own. My husband is in the merchant navy. North Atlantic. He gets very little leave, so it'll be good to have someone about the place.'

'My brother is in the navy,' I said.

'Oh really. Their paths might cross without ever knowing.'

My landlady stared at her empty cup for a moment. *She misses him.*

'Another cup?'

'Yes please.'

'Homemade,' she announced as she put a plate of thick brown biscuits between us. 'Ginger. Please help yourself.'

The biscuits were delicious; it was all that I could do to resist polishing off the lot.

'Very good,' I mumbled between mouthfuls.

'Your letter stated that you'll be working nights.'

'Apparently, yes.'

'We'll have to work out some sort of routine, Miss Mewer.'

'Please call me Jean.'

'Very well, Jean. We'll have to think about meals and so on, to fit in with your shifts.'

'I have to be there on Monday morning to sort things out I imagine. Then my first night shift will be Tuesday night. Shall we talk about mealtimes when I've finished on Monday? I'll know what's what by then.'

'I hope that you'll sleep during the day. It's a quiet road. We've had a lot of raids, mostly up at the factories near the canal, near where you'll be. A good few bombs missed the works and destroyed houses here and there. Nothing in our road yet, touch wood.'

48

My landlady managed a weak smile. Perhaps she was trying to cheer me up after all the talk about air raids and bombs.

'The coal man comes on a Monday morning. You'll probably hear him clattering about.'

'I'm sure I'll be fine,' I said.

'Let me show you your room.'

'There are two bedrooms. The bathroom is along there. You're at the back. Quieter,' said my landlady as I followed her upstairs.

'There's a one-bar electric fire for the winter. Otherwise, it's what you see. There's plenty of space for your things. Come down when you're settled and we'll see about tea.'

I hope that means something to eat.

'Oh, I'll show you how to use the blackouts. My husband made them. You have to put them up at night.'

My room was spacious, larger than the garret I slept in at the doctor's, probably the largest bedroom I have ever used in my whole life.

I wonder whose room this was.

There was just enough space to squeeze behind the dressing table to look out of the window.

I wonder if her husband put up the shelter.

An Anderson shelter occupied a space at the end of a long narrow garden, beyond a vegetable plot. I had seen photographs of them in the newspapers back home; the real thing looked very small. How it was meant to protect you from falling bombs struck me as a mystery.[11]

---

[11] A structure based on galvanised corrugated steel panels, designed to protect a family of up to six people, issued or sold to households depending on their income.

I turned back into my room and opened my suitcase on the rug, avoiding putting it on the pink counterpane.

So far, so good.

My room was spotless, well-furnished, and smelt of lavender from something unseen. If this was to be my home for the duration, then I have struck lucky: a nice room and a friendly landlady. What a contrast from the harsh treatment meted out by Mrs Robertson.

I placed my personal things on the lace dressing table cover, emptied my case and stored it on top of the wardrobe.

I wonder when I'll next use it.

I spent Sunday morning looking around the immediate area. There was a row of shops at the end of Church Road and larger shops in the High Street, near where I got off the bus the day before.

Mrs Ellsworth drew a map showing me how to walk to the factory, a distance of about a mile and a half.

I timed the walk on Sunday afternoon. I wanted to be sure to arrive early the next morning.

Chapter Five

First Days

I joined a group of anxious-looking women waiting outside the entrance to an office block in Heath Street.

'Are you waiting to start today?' I asked them.

'Are you?' one of them replied.

'Yes.'

'I'm a bit scared,' she added.

'Me too,' said another.

After introducing ourselves to one another, Monica, Viv, Doreen and me were asked inside by a well-dressed young woman and shown into a dreary room that resembled a classroom.

'Help yourselves to a cup of tea,' said the woman. 'Someone will be with you shortly.'

The four of us took our cups of tea and sat nervously at two of the tables at the front of the classroom.

'What happens next?' whispered Viv.

Her question was answered when a tall woman wearing a tweed suit and thickly framed glasses bustled into the room and stood imperiously before us, eyeing us critically.

'Welcome to our works, ladies,' she began. 'My name is Mrs Frobisher, Head of Personnel. The purpose of this morning is to enrol you as employees and explain what your work here will involve. Firstly, what do we do for the war effort here …'

Mrs Frobisher explained about our shifts, what we will have to wear, how we will learn our work, and many other things about procedures. My head felt at bursting point, filled with so much information.

'… and the red light means go to the shelters. Only on red, is that clear? We work through most air raids because of the work that we do here. Any questions?'

We were all too overwhelmed to ask anything.

'I'm sure that you will have questions later. Listen, pay close attention, and watch, and you won't go far wrong.'

Mrs Frobisher paused to let her words sink in.

'Your contribution to the war effort here will be highly valued. Good accurate work will be expected of you. In turn, you will be well paid, probably better paid than in your previous jobs.'

We exchanged glances amongst ourselves.

'Next. To practical matters.'

We were told about punctuality, clocking in and out, break times, and blackouts.

'For the two of you on nights, Miss Muir and Miss Bishop, the factory is completely blacked-out at night. We have to be very careful that even the tiniest bit of light does not leak out. After you have completed some forms, I'll show you where things are.'

'Are we the only ones starting today?' asked Doreen Bishop.

'Yes. We don't anticipate any more new war workers for the time being.'

We were shown the cloakroom where we would change into our work clothes: overalls, rubber shoes, and hair turbans. We were each provided with a locker, a key for it, and an enamel brooch with our clock card number printed on it.

'Wear it on your overalls at all times,' instructed Mrs Frobisher. 'This makes it easier to record your work for pay purposes.'

I wondered if my new work colleagues also didn't understand what this meant, as I hung my overalls in my locker and put the enamel brooch on the shelf.

The long wooden bench along the length of the cloakroom between its two rows of lockers enabled us to try on our rubber shoes.

'Does anyone need to try on another size of shoe or overalls?' asked Mrs Frobisher. 'No, all right.'

An official-looking woman appeared.

'Miss Jones and Miss Jenkins: would you go with my colleague. Miss Muir and Miss Bishop: please follow me.'

Doreen and I followed the tweed suit out of the rear of the office block, across the wide yard towards a long, low building.

'Before we go into the machine shop, I must warn you that it is very, very noisy. You won't be able to hear me. Watch and follow. Stop when I stop and note what I point to. Keep your questions until we are outside again.'

Our leader pushed open a wooden door, crossed a wide vestibule and stopped before what looked like rubber doors, each with a small window at head height. The noise of the machine shop, as she called it, could be heard thrumming loudly beyond the doors. Mrs Frobisher pushed at one of them and ushered us through ahead of her.

My hands flew to cover my ears in an attempt to lessen the immense wall of sound that confronted us.

Dozens of machines, their shiny steel components rattling and whirring, shook the air in a deafening cacophony. Unfamiliar smells filled what was left of the air space in the huge machine shop. The sight and sound of where I would be at work overwhelmed me completely.

'Jean, Jean … are you all right?'

I opened my eyes; Doreen's kindly face slowly came into focus. 'What happened?'

'Just lie still please,' said a nurse. 'You're in the FAP.'

'The factory's First Aid Post, Jean,' said Doreen. 'You fainted, flat out. Someone caught you. Otherwise, you would've hit your head on the hard floor.'

'Fainted! Oh dear, they won't want me now, will they?'

'Don't you worry,' said the nurse. 'You're not the first. You'll get used to it.'

'I'll wait outside,' said Doreen.

The nurse kept an eye on me until I felt ready to sit on the edge of the couch that I had been lying on.

'Slowly now. Can you stand?' she said.

I took another sip of water, stood rather unsteadily and took a few steps across the tiny first aid room.

'And back again,' suggested the nurse.

After a few more steps back and forth, I felt confident enough to continue.

'I've got to try again, going in there I mean,' I said to the nurse. 'If I can't do this, they'll send me home. I hope that they'll let me try again.'

Mrs Frobisher's assistant put her head around the door. 'Ah, Miss Muir. You're on your feet. How do you feel?'

'Much better, thank you. I'm sorry I fainted.'

'It happens from time to time. I'm Miss Franks, by the way. I work for Mrs Frobisher. Are you ready to be shown round the shop?'

'Yes, I'm ready.'

I must do this.

Doreen and I followed Miss Franks until we were standing outside the rubber doors again. 'Remember, stop when I stop. Observe what I point to,' she told us. 'Keep your questions until later.'

I took a deep breath and entered the machine shop, letting the din envelop me, determined not to fail this time.

The doors gave way to the end of several lines of machines, which I found out later were mostly lathes. Some kind of engine at the door end of each line seemed to be turning shafts high above the rows of lathes where Miss Franks pointed. What looked to me like long belts suspended from each shaft whizzed around, giving movement to each piece of machinery.

The engine and belt mechanisms generated most of the noise, or at least it seemed that way from where we stood near the doors to the machine shop.

We followed Miss Franks until she stopped in front of a bank of clocks. She waved a blank card to show us what a clocking-in and clocking-out card looked like. Large slotted wooden noticeboards were positioned either side of each clock: one labelled "In" and the other labelled "Out".

Miss Franks posted the blank card in an empty "Out" slot, then she placed it in a large slit in one of the clocks and pressed a short lever, removed the card and placed it an empty slot on the "In" board. She passed the card to Doreen and me to show where the correct time had been stamped on the card. Miss Franks showed us the procedure once more.

So that's take your card from there, stamp it in there and put it in the other side.

Miss Franks pointed to a large lamp placed high on the wall above the clocks. It glowed white.

I wonder what it's for.

We followed Miss Franks along one of the rows of lathes. Women in grey overalls and hair coverings worked with alarming speed and dexterity, flipping levers and turning handles, their bodies bent over pieces of steel doused with what for all the world looked like milk.

God, I'll never learn how to do this.

Miss Franks stopped at one of the lathes. The female operator intent on her work in front of us didn't look up from what she was doing while we gazed in wonder as she guided a cutting tool across a circular bar of steel that was gripped by her machine, sending spirals of grey steel floating this way and that as she worked on the piece of metal so that it changed shape before our eyes.

I became mesmerised by the skill of her hands, by the way they were in command of her lathe. Even the din of the machine shop faded a little as we watched.

After more passes across her piece of work, it appeared to break off. She handed it to Miss Franks after letting the milky stuff flow over it for a few seconds.

To cool it down?

Miss Franks held up what looked like a large bolt before handing it for us to examine. It felt quite hot.

Miss Franks nodded to the lathe operator and handed the finished piece back to her. She smiled briefly and mouthed something that I took to be "thanks".

I saw her put the bolt in a box of identical bolts, wipe her hands on a rag, and enter something on a card.

We followed Miss Franks to the other end of the row of lathes, then back along the next row.

I quickly got the impression of many similar-looking machines engaged in similar tasks. Presumably Doreen and I would be shown how to operate a lathe: otherwise, why show us the shop?

Back in the vestibule, the rubber doors shut out some of the racket beyond.

I breathed heavily with relief.

'You all right, Jean?' asked Doreen.

I nodded.

Survived.

Back in the classroom, we had some questions.

'Your clock cards will be already in place when you arrive for your first shift tomorrow evening,' replied Miss Franks in response to my first question. 'The card rack is arranged numerically, so just look for your card, stamp it and put it in the correct slot on the "In" board.

'I'm glad you asked me about the lamp, Miss Muir,' Miss Franks said when I asked my next question. 'You wouldn't have been able to hear my explanation in the shop. White means that there are no air raids taking place. Blue is a public alert for the benefit of the surrounding area. We work through these raids. Red is an emergency: we evacuate to the bomb shelters during these.'

Doreen broke the silence as we took in the explanation about the significance of the lamp. 'How will we learn how to operate one of those machines?' she pleaded. 'It looks really hard.'

'You will both be assigned to someone who you will watch and learn from. They will be expecting you at six-thirty tomorrow evening. You'll be with Molly, Miss Muir, and Miss Bishop with Ivy. It'll all become clear as you go along. It's not as difficult or complicated as it looks at first sight.'

Doreen puffed her cheeks out noisily.

'Is it all women?' I asked. 'I saw a few men walking around.'

'Machine operators are exclusively women,' replied Miss Franks. 'Some of them are local, like Molly. Others are war workers such as yourselves. The men set up the lathes and get them ready for you and they deal with any faults and the like.

'To begin with, you will be paid a basic wage. Later, you'll be able to add to this with piece work.'

'"Peace work!" Sorry, I'm a bit confused,' said Doreen. 'I thought this was war work.'

'"Piece" as in a piece of something, something that you make, like the bolt you saw,' explained Miss Franks. 'You earn a bonus depending on how many good quality pieces, screws or bolts say, that you make.'

'Oh, of course, I see. Silly me,' said Doreen. 'So, you have to work quickly.'

'Balanced and measured against quality,' said Miss Franks. 'You'll soon see how it works when you watch over the next day or two.'

'Won't Molly lose money while she's teaching me?' I asked.

'We've taken that into consideration while you learn, Miss Muir. Molly is a very good lathe operator, and she is an excellent teacher. Learn well. You're in good hands, both of you.

'I suggest that you both have some lunch in the works canteen before you leave for the day. There isn't anything else that we need to do today. Your shift is six-thirty to six-thirty, starting tomorrow evening. Be here in plenty of time to get changed and clock-in.'

'This week we start on Tuesday,' said Doreen. 'Would you remind me what the normal week is please.'

'Sunday night to Friday night. You don't come in after six-thirty on a Saturday morning until six-thirty in the evening the next day. In other words, you get Saturday night off.'

'Phew,' exclaimed Doreen.

'All right, then. I'll show you where the canteen is. You might find the others there.'

The four of us talked at once, excitedly, and nervously at one end of one of the long tables in the canteen, conspicuous in our everyday clothes.

'When're you starting?' asked a woman in work clothes who was sitting with her workmates near to us.

'Tomorrow morning.'

'Tomorrow night.'

'Good luck, she said, gathering up her used cutlery.

The canteen soon emptied. One thirty must be the end of the lunch break for the day shift.

'It's going to be odd eating dinner at one o'clock in the morning, Jean,' said Doreen. 'Not sure I'll get used to that.'

'Can't you ask to switch to days,' said Monica.

'Dunno. I'll see how it goes,' replied Doreen.

'You all right with nights, Jean?' asked Viv.

'I suppose so. I don't know how they decided. I'll go along with it,' I replied.

'Don't suppose we'll see much of you two from now on,' added Monica.

Doreen and I exchanged glances.

'I don't suppose so,' I said.

We wished one another good luck and tried to find the way out onto Heath Street.

'I walk from here,' I said to Doreen.

'Bus at the top of the High Street for me,' she replied.

'Well, that's it. We're in now. See you tomorrow evening then.'

'Until then, Jean. Hope you're feeling all right.'

'Aye. I'm fine thanks. Bye.'

'Bye.'

My landlady was out at work, so I let myself in with the key she had given me, went directly upstairs, took off my shoes and lay on the bed. My head still rang with the whirring sound of dozens of lathes as I lay staring at the ceiling, longing to turn the volume in my head down.

After a few moments, I fell asleep despite the tumult between my ears.

I arrived at six o'clock the following evening, opened my locker and took out my overalls. The room soon became crowded with women coming off the day shift, some standing in their undergarments in the throes of changing into their everyday clothes, mingling with other women changing out of their everyday clothes.

I felt rather self-conscious. I had never shared a room with other women in a state of semi-undress. The sight of so many women stripping off their overalls, taking no notice of me helped me to overcome my initial embarrassment.

I folded my skirt and blouse, put them on the shelf in my locker, and hung my summer coat on the hook at the back.

As I was tying my hair turban, a short woman with black curly hair approached. 'Here, let me show you a better way to tie it.'

'Thanks,' I said. 'I had a practice yesterday.'

'You've nearly got it. There.'

She stood back, admiring her effort. 'Are you Jean?'

'Yes.'

'I'm Molly. I'll be looking after you … getting you started. This is Jean, girls,' Molly called out.

A chorus of "Hello, Jean" accompanied by arm waving identified Molly's "girls".

'Thanks for looking after me, Molly. This is all so new to me.'

'You won't be able to hear me in there,' warned Molly. 'Watch what I do. I'll go slowly to begin with. Save your questions for break time. You'll soon learn how to lip read. Ready?'

I pinned my number badge to the front of my overalls and followed Molly to the machine shop.

'Make something special for Hitler,' called out one of Molly's pals as we left the locker room.

'It doesn't stop him coming over at nights,' muttered Molly.

The wall of sound hit me the instant Molly pushed open the door to the machine shop.

I'll get used to it.

I followed Molly to her lathe, where she motioned me to go around and watch from the other side.

Molly spent a few minutes inspecting her lathe, giving it a few wipes here and there with a piece of rag that she spirited from somewhere. Soon she seemed satisfied with how the previous operator had left her machine.

Next, Molly beckoned to a man who was standing near the next lathe. He pointed to his wrist, indicating two minutes with his fingers.

He must be one of the setters they told us about yesterday.

Molly continued wiping her lathe until the man came over.

Molly mouthed something to me: his name, probably.

I'll ask her later.

Molly's setter made some adjustments to the large upper section of her lathe, took something out, looked at it, then replaced it.

He said something to Molly, glanced at me and moved along to another lathe.

Molly mouthed something to me, which I took to be "watch". She pointed to her eyes, then pointed downwards again. "Watch" she mouthed again.

Here goes.

I couldn't see how she started her lathe. It whirred into action, adding to the din surrounding me.

Molly pointed to the belt that drove the part of the lathe to my right that spun a short rod of steel that she had inserted before she switched on.

The steel rod turned at enormous speed.

Next, Molly set a stream of thin milky-white fluid cascading onto the rod.

She mouthed what looked like "ooh".

Cool. Keeps it cool.

Molly then turned a long lever and part of the large upper section of her lathe moved gradually along the bar of steel.

This is like I saw yesterday.

Unwanted steel spiralled upwards and sideways until Molly was satisfied.

How do you know when to …

Molly flipped the lever and drew the cutting tool away from the rod before engaging the next tool. This one cut a thread.

Why didn't it cut more off like the first tool?

The transition from a shiny, smooth rod of steel to one with a spiral thread looked like magic. Yet Molly had achieved this in just a few minutes with the flip of a lever or two.

The next stage seemed to repeat the second, before Molly did something with another tool that snapped off the finished piece.

Molly beckoned me to watch from her side.

She handed me the still slightly hot finished bolt.

'I'll never remember all that,' I shouted in her ear.

'You will,' she shouted back. 'Keep watching.'

I stood next to Molly while she made the next bolt.

First, she turns that, then this, then … gosh, will I ever learn all this?

I spent the time until the break watching, swapping sides to vary the view of Molly's movements. Gradually I began to memorise the sequence of the cutting tools she engaged and the order of the levers and wheels that she brought into action.

By the time a shrill hooter sounded for tea break, Molly had accumulated neat rows of shiny, finished bolts laid out in a wooden box. She pointed to a record sheet attached to a clipboard suspended from a screw sticking out from her lathe at waist height.

'Don't forget to copy your numbers into your book,' Molly told me over a cup of tea and a bun in the canteen.

'They haven't given me one yet,' I replied.

'They will, once you're on your own.'

I wonder when that will be?

'What d'yer think of it so far, Jean?' said Peggy, one of Molly's pals.

'It looks complicated,' I replied. 'I've never seen anything like it.'

'A real country girl, then,' said Lil, Peggy's neighbour at the long table in the canteen. 'Welcome to Brum, the city Hitler loves to keep on bombing.'

'You'll soon get the hang of it,' said Peggy. 'We all did.'

'Uh oh, there's the hooter. Back to it, ladies,' said Lil.

I followed their example and put my used mug and plate on the end of the counter.

'You alright for cash, Jean?' said Molly, as we filed out of the canteen. 'Until pay day, I mean.'

'I'm fine thanks, Molly. Saved a bit up from my previous job.'

'I'll go a bit quicker for the next stretch, just so you can see my normal working speed. Signal for me to slow down if you want. Dinner's at half past midnight.'

I began to feel drowsy even in a standing position, during what seemed an age until the hooter sounded for the hour break for what Molly had called "dinner".

In the middle of the night.

I ate a sandwich with my landlady in the late afternoon as part of our arrangement She would provide afternoon tea after I got up and breakfast when I got in from work. I had let her know that I would get my main meal of the day in the canteen.

'I couldn't eat dinner in the middle of the night,' she had said.

'You can get a meat and two veg dinner for about a bob,' Molly told me as we queued in the canteen.[12]

The noise of clattering trays and chattering voices came as a blessed relief from the unremitting racket of the machine shop. An hour away from the din, sitting down to eat and chat dampened my drowsiness.

At least I'm standing. Molly is bent all the while.

I wondered how long it would take me to make an aircraft bolt and worried if I could get used to bending for hours on end.

'All right, Jean?' came a voice behind ne.

'Oh, hello, Doreen,' I replied. 'How's it going?'

'I'm way down the other end of the shop from you. It's okay, there's a lot to learn, isn't there? See you later, Jean,' said Doreen as she carried her tray to another table.

'We started together,' I explained to our table. 'I noticed a blue light on the way out. Has there been a raid?'

'Probably, Jean,' replied Lil. 'We never hear anything unless it's really near. We'll find out when we clock off in the morning.'

'Have you ever had to go to the shelter?' I asked.

'A few times during the blitz,' replied Peggy.

'Blitz?'

---

[12] Five pence Sterling in today's money.

'Brum was badly hit in the months before you came. Last winter was the worst. Mostly we worked on through it.'

'There are still raids,' said Molly. 'Not so many, but they still go on. We're safe enough until the red goes on, then we're off to the shelter.'

'There hasn't been a red raid for weeks,' said Peggy.

'Are we a target because of what we make?' I asked.

'That we are,' replied Molly. 'Hitler'll love to bomb us out, slow down production of planes. Hasn't yet though.'

'We're invincible,' suggested Lil. 'He can't find us.'

'He might hear us,' I replied. 'It's the noisiest place I've ever been in, the shop I mean.'

'You'll get used to it,' said Lil and Peggy in unison.

'I'm going to try my best,' I said.

'C'mon, ladies,' said Molly when the hooter sounded. 'Back to telling Hitler to bugger off.'

Immediately after the dinner break, Molly motioned to me to stand next to her while she went through the operations of making a bolt very slowly, all the while commenting on what she was doing with the various levers and other parts of her lathe. I couldn't hear much of what she said, but I tried to match what I could hear with the movement of her lips.

I had been told that I would have to learn how to lip read and surprised myself that it would take me only a few days to begin to get the hang of it. A combination of sign language and lip reading would soon become enough to communicate with Molly and with Stan, our long-suffering setter.

My first night shift dragged to a close at six-thirty in the morning, after spending the best part of eleven hours watching and marvelling at Molly's skill. She had been very patient with me, explaining, pointing, working slowly then quickly, then slowly again: she was a good teacher.

I struggled to stifle yet another yawn as we changed in the locker room.

'So, what do you think about going solo?' asked Molly.

'Tonight?'

'I'll stand over you. You'll learn better that way. Don't worry, I'll keep an eye on you.'

'All right, I'm game,' I said.

'Good for you,' said Molly. 'Once I've seen what you can do on your own, we'll decide when you can work unsupervised. See you tonight.'

''Till later,' I said.

Leaving the factory into the early light of a May morning was a shock. The machine shop was completely blacked out day and night. The artificial light threw a greenish yellow hue over everything and everyone. Faces looked ghostly and pale, as if an illness had spread and affected all without exception.

I blinked into the daylight as I began the walk to my digs. The short walk from the machine shop to the building with the locker room and canteen hadn't been sufficient to get used to daylight. I saw no evidence of last night's air raid.

I wonder where it happened.

I stood nervously next to Molly shortly after six-thirty that evening. This time I stood in the operator's position, with Molly at my side.

'Ready, Jean?' she mouthed.

I nodded.

Well, here goes. Remember the steps.

I took a bar of steel from the box, tightened it in the chuck and switched on. The chuck picked up speed almost immediately, but the cascade of suds seemed to spray all over the place.

Bad start.

Molly showed me how to adjust the flow.

Now for the first cut.

I turned the long lever to select the correct tool from the lathe's turret, turned the wheel, and began to make my first cut.[13]

Nothing happened at first.

Molly pointed.

The tip wasn't in contact with the steel rod. A little further; still nothing. Then it happened: spirals of steel came away.

Turn the wheel back now.

Molly nodded.

Now for the next bit with the other tool.

The machine's setting miraculously cut a thread.

'Too slow,' mouthed Molly.

I could see that the thread looked all wrong.

'Start again,' I lip-read.

Molly put my first attempt in the waste steel bin; I started again.

It took me a few attempts to get the thread correct.

Now to make the head and cut it off.

I snapped it!

'You should have seen my first,' Molly told me at the tea break.

---

[13] The (capstan) lathe's turret holds several different cutting tools capable of performing different operations.

I spent the first half of my shift practising repeatedly, with Molly hand-signalling, showing me adjustments and encouraging me to keep trying.

By dinner time, I had produced half a dozen bolts to Molly's satisfaction. Jack the inspector passed the one he examined with his micrometer and thread checker. He gave me a thumbs up before he moved on to the next lathe.

After dinner break, Jack moved me to the vacant lathe next to Molly; it had been set up by Stan ready for me to start work on my own.

'I'll be right next to you, Jean. Call me over if you need help,' Molly told me in the canteen.

This is it. Time to prove myself.

'Go slowly. Don't worry about how many. Go slow and make 'em good,' said Molly as we entered the shop, its strange light and relentless din enveloped me as I took my place.

Lil gave me a thumbs up from the next row.

Here goes.

Chapter Six

Factory Worker

The second half of the shift saw me throw quite a few pieces into the waste metal bin, as well as place several completed bolts in my "out" box.

Jack rejected several on sight but accepted most of my first set of aircraft screws, following his visual inspection and measurements.

'Keep at your own pace,' advised Molly at the ten past four tea break. 'Accuracy is the order of the day. Piece rate bonuses will come later.'

'Thanks, Molly. I'm slowly getting the hang of it,' I said.

'You'll be all right,' she said. 'Did you see the blue light?'

'No.'

'Me neither,' said Lil. 'I wonder who got it last night,' she continued, as if talking to herself.

I had watched Molly clear up just prior to the end of yesterday's shift, so I knew what to do. It was vital to leave our lathes clean and ready for the day shift.

Surfaces were wiped with a large piece of rag, which was put in a bin for reuse. Each lathe was provided with a small brush, used to sweep swarf onto the floor.[14] Either Angus, the elderly labourer from Glasgow, or James with the film star looks and too

---

[14] Waste metal as a result of turning steel in a lathe.

young to be in the forces, kept the floor spotless and free of swarf throughout the night shift.

Angus and I exchanged a few words, despite my rudimentary lip-reading ability; someone must have told him that I came from Scotland. James always reddened when he swept around our area. He often looked embarrassed even without knowing what was said if one of the girls mouthed something; James's lip-reading skills weren't up to much.

'Who're you going home with today, James?' mouthed Lil as he swept around our feet at the end of the shift. 'You can sweep up my swarf any old time,' she added.

The machine shop was not as noisy with all the lathes shutting down, so he must have heard the end-of-shift comments aimed at him.

'Wouldn't you just love to mother him,' said Peggy as she cleared up her lathe.

'Do something to him,' replied Lil with a knowing laugh.

I didn't join in with their ribbing but thanked James when he had cleared the last of my swarf.

'Is my lathe okay?' I asked Molly. We could just about hear ourselves above the noise of dozens of lathes slowing down.

'Perfect,' she replied. 'Have a look at how the day shift operator leaves it ready for tonight. I can see that you like to be neat and thorough.'

'Jack passed several of my first efforts,' I told Molly while we changed.

'You'll learn fast, Jean,' she said. 'I can tell already. Remember, concentrate on the basics. You won't be on a piece rate just yet.'

The result of last night's blue light met me as I crossed the High Street on my way to my digs. Two shop fronts had been destroyed, their remains strewn across the pavement and onto the road. Bricks, glass, and lengths of splintered wood forced the few citizens who were out and about at seven in the morning to walk down the middle of the road.

As I picked my way past piles of rubble, two ARP wardens carried a stretcher across the road in front of me.[15] I could have reached out and touched the edge of the bloodied and dusty covering of what I assumed to be a body, whose shape beneath its barely adequate cover was much shorter than the stretcher.

A child. Dead or alive?

I couldn't move from where I stood in the middle of the High Street.

The destruction of buildings was hard enough to contemplate getting used to; the loss of life was too much to bear. My first sight of blood spilled during a night of bombing left me rigid with shock.

'Move along, love,' barked another ARP warden, his protective helmet askew.

'Sorry,' I mumbled.

Another stretcher emerged from the remains of the shattered shop, its bearers climbing then descending the heaps of rubble on their way to an ambulance parked across the street.

'Sorry,' I repeated. 'It's just that I've never seen …'

---

[15] An Air Raid Precautions (ARP) warden's main task was to protect citizens during air raids.

'Get used to it, pet,' said one of the ARP wardens. 'It happens a lot round here, on account of the works near the canal. Where've you been anyway?'

'I work nights. We don't hear a thing.'

'Well just you take care. Mind the glass.'

'Okay, thanks.'

I walked slowly to my digs, unable to shift the sight of the child's shroud from my mind.

I hope that my brothers and sisters are safe at home.

∗

Dinner time on the Friday night shift at the end of my first week began as a noticeably jolly affair: there was no shift on Saturdays.

'The firm organises entertainment on the second and fourth Saturday of the month,' said Peggy. 'It's a dance tomorrow. Comin', Jean?'

'Ooh, yes, I'd love to. I haven't got a dress though.'

'Buy yourself one this afternoon. There's a good womenswear shop at the top of the High Street. Go on, treat yourself.'

'If it's still there. Some shops were bombed, weren't they,' I said.

'Two kids killed. Blown out of their beds in the flat above one of the shops,' said Lil, her voice quivering with anger.

'I saw one of the bodies on a stretcher,' I said. 'It was a very sad sight.'

'Your first then?' asked Peggy.

I nodded.

'Might not be your last I'm afraid to say, Jean,' said Molly, between mouthfuls of mashed potato. 'Birmingham has suffered. Its citizens have. The worst of the bombing might be over, but there's still death and destruction. Since France fell, Hitler's been bombing the hell out of us.'

'Sorry, it's my fault,' I said. 'Sorry to have mentioned it. It's just that someone mentioned the dress shop.'

'Well, let's have a good night tomorrow,' said Lil. 'No Luftwaffe ain't goin' to stop us.'

'You haven't been paid yet,' whispered Molly on our way back to the machine shop. 'Can you afford a dress for the dance?'

'Yes, I can,' I replied. 'I'm looking forward to it. Oh, are there any men apart from the ones we know?'

'A few. Either too old or too young to fight.'

'Or too ugly,' chimed Lil from behind us.

'Or too shy, like James,' added Peggy.

I went straight to bed after breakfast, intent on getting up early in the afternoon, leaving enough time to go and buy a dress.

'The local shop'll be closed,' said Mrs Ellsworth. 'Saturday half-day closing. You could go into the city centre, what's left of it.'

I had brought my one and only dress from home. I decided to wear it rather than catching a bus into the centre of Birmingham. I had seen enough bombed-out buildings for one day. A visit to a department store in the city centre could be put off for another day.

'We'll go together next Saturday,' suggested my landlady. 'Arthur gets some leave soon. I'd like something new too. We'll make a day of it.'

I wouldn't be paid until the end of my second week. Working a week in hand meant that I wouldn't be able to send a postal order home and kit myself out with a new dress just yet.[16] My old dress would just have to do.

---

[16] A postal order (PO) is a type of money order usually intended for sending money through the mail. It is purchased at a post office and is payable at another post office to the named recipient.

Chapter Seven

After the Dance is Over

'Yer a fine dancer, Jean,' said Molly. 'Where'd you learn to dance like that?'

'Village dances at home. Our main entertainment. I missed them while I was working away from home though, which was most of the time actually.'

The members of the band clustered around the bar, enjoying a smoke and a drink during their break. One of the saxophone players approached our table.

'We usually hold a competition for the best dancer of the night,' he said, directing his remark to me. 'There's no prize. It's just a bit of fun.'

'We need to find a bloke who can match Jean,' said Molly.

'Not many of them around here,' said Peggy.

'Well, see what you can do,' said the saxophonist. 'We start again soon. Hope to see you ladies dancing.'

'With each other, mostly,' said Peggy. 'I haven't had hold of a man for ages.'

The whole table erupted with loud laughter, drawing the attention of adjacent tables, and knowing looks from everyone standing at the bar.

The saxophone player shook his head, grinned from ear to ear and re-joined his bandmates at the bar.

'My round,' announced Molly.

I went with Molly to help her with the drinks. A tray each would keep us going for a few more numbers from Sydney and his excellent dance band.

'Thanks, Moll,' everyone chorused as we emptied our trays of glasses and bottles.

'How're yer enjoying yer first works dance, Jean?" asked Madge.

'Very much. It's good that we can do this and maintain the blackouts.'

'They're a good firm to work for,' added Madge. 'They look after you. The entertainment is good for morale, that's what I reckon.'

'You're right there, Madge,' I replied. 'It's a nice break from the long shifts.'

'Are you picking up the work, learning like?' continued Madge.

'Molly's a good teacher,' I said. 'I'm getting there, I think.'

'She taught me,' said Madge. 'She's a good one. Hey up, she's coming back from the ladies.'

'We can stop talking about her now,' I whispered.

'Jean, you've got an admirer,' announced Madge.

I turned to find Jack, one of the night shift inspectors, standing over my chair.

'May I have the next dance, Miss Muir,' he said, with a polite smile.

Jack danced the foxtrot expertly; we jelled as a dance couple almost immediately. Despite his ample bulk, Jack was a nimble and considerate lead. During the quickstep that followed, we whirled around the dance floor to the admiring glances of other couples, our movements encouraging them to give way, affording us more space.

Towards the end of the number, everyone moved to the edge of the floor, forcing others out of their seats to watch us: the only couple on the floor.

I suddenly felt very self-conscious, aware that the gaze of everyone fell upon Jack and me.

Jack beamed as he spun me skilfully to the rapid tempo of the dance. I anticipated most of his improvisations; no one seemed to notice any that I missed.

The members of the band joined in the applause as Jack led me to our table.

'And the winners are Jack and Jean,' announced the band leader.

'Thank you, Miss Muir,' he said, bowing smartly. 'You dance very well indeed.'

'You too, Mr Harper.'

'Please call me Jack, when we're not at work I mean.'

I nodded.

'I'll say goodnight.'

'Goodnight … Jack.'

'Blimey, you two,' exclaimed Molly. 'He's a bit different when he's off duty.'

'I'll say,' added Madge. 'Moves well for a big man.'

'Time we were off,' said Molly.

A few of the women partnered up for the last waltz, while we finished the last of our drinks.

'He failed a batch of mine last week,' complained Lil.

'Just doing his job,' suggested Molly. 'C'mon girls.'

We waited until it sounded like the lobby was empty before we stepped into its pale light, closing the light of the canteen-cum-dance floor behind us. A quick exit into the yard minimised escaping light to a level that still managed to annoy the ARP warden. How else were we supposed to leave the building?

You can't dance in the dark.

'Walk you home, Miss Muir?' came Jack's voice out of the darkness behind us.

'No, thank you. I'm alright.'

'Are you sure?'

'Yes thanks.'

'Okay.'

I heard the disappointment in his single word reply.

Dancing's one thing.

'Night, Jean,' chorused the girls.

'Night, all.'

'Great dancing, Jean,' I heard as we went our separate ways out of the factory gate.

Jack wasn't there at the start of the dance a month later. I was relieved that we wouldn't become the centre of attention.

It couldn't happen again, could it?

I danced with Lil a few times; none of the few men present seemed willing to ask me.

Oh dear, they must think me hoity toity.

Towards the end of the evening, Jack appeared. He made directly for our table and asked me to dance the last waltz.

The dance was an unpleasant experience: he had been drinking. He held me too tightly and breathed beery fumes into my face.

'Walk you home, Miss Muir,' he blurted out the instant that the music stopped.

'Thank you, no, Mr Harper,' I said firmly, returning to our table.

'I'm off now, girls,' I said, pulling my coat from the back of my chair.

'You alright, Jean?' asked Molly as we made to leave.

'He stinks of drink,' I whispered, 'and won't take no for an answer.'

'C'mon, Jean. I'll walk you to the gate,' said Molly. 'That'll keep him away.'

'He might be a good dancer, but he's a hopeless suitor,' I remarked.

'We could all see that he has his eye on you,' said Molly. 'What'll you do?'

'Tell him I'm engaged if he asks to walk me home again.'

'Good idea. Goodnight, Jean. You look after yourself now.'

"Night, Molly. Thank you for looking out for me.'

'See you tomorrow evening. Another week awaits.'

It took only a few seconds for Molly's footsteps to fade into the blackness of the street that swallowed her.

I followed the white stripes painted on the kerbs along my familiar route to my digs, narrowly avoiding bumping into people making their way along the pitch-dark streets. The walk to my digs gave me an opportunity to reflect on what had happened earlier in the evening.

I had remarked to Molly on Jack Harper's lack of skill as a suitor as if I knew what I had been talking about. On the contrary, for the first time in my life a man had taken an interest in me. I was confused, rather frightened and uncertain what to do about it other than claim to be engaged.

What started as a thoroughly enjoyable dance a month ago had turned into disappointment. The things that brought me happiness – nattering with the girls and dancing – a release from the noise, long hours and hard work might have to come to an end to avoid a man's attention. The very thought made me feel sad as I trudged through the darkness.

I certainly had a lot to learn about the opposite sex. Working as a domestic servant had given me a sheltered life, a life dominated by providing long hours of service with very little time off for socialising. Here I was, in my mid-twenties never having given romance more than a fleeting thought that it might happen to me one day.

Not with Jack Harper, that's for certain.

I reached my digs in a state of low spirits, not how I expected to feel after a night out with my new friends.

During the intervening month between my first two dance evenings, I had gradually become quicker and proficient as a lathe operator. The first shift after I rebuffed Jack Harper for a second time found me transferred from the basic rate to pay with a piece rate bonus.

'You'll be fine, Jean,' Molly told me in the locker room. 'Don't rush and don't worry if your bonus is low to begin with. We all started that way.'

'Jack Harper is one of the inspectors. I'm a bit bothered,' I said, tying my turban.

'He's usually at the other end of the shop from us though. Don't you worry, Jean. Your work will speak for itself.'

After the dinner break, Jack Harper appeared unexpectedly on our line. I carried on working, trying to ignore him politely as he measured a sample of my completed bolts taken from the top of my box. He gestured to me to stop what I was doing.

'I've had to fail some of these, Miss Muir,' I lip-read. 'Carry on please.'

I glanced across at Molly; she glared at the inspector's back as he walked away with my box of completed work.

When he returned a few minutes later, my box was half empty.

'What's wrong with them?' I mouthed.

'Not accurate enough,' is what I thought I lip-read before he walked away without another word.

Molly looked at me, flung her wiping-round rag down and switched off her lathe just at the instant that the hooter sounded for the tea break.

'What was all that about, Jean?' Molly asked, sipping her tea noisily.

'He's failed a whole batch, evidently,' I replied.

'The other inspector, Arthur whatshisname, passed all your work all of last week. So, what's changed? Nothing,' said Molly, answering her own question. 'I know what this is about,' she added, banging her teacup on its saucer.

'So do I,' I said. 'I'm sorry to be the cause of trouble.'

'Not a bit of it,' said Peggy.

'It's not your fault,' added Lil.

'Men, eh,' muttered Molly. 'I've got a plan,' she added, tapping her nose with a finger.

The same thing happened just before the dinner break on Monday's shift.

Molly wolfed down her faggots and peas, eager to tell me her plan. 'The next time he does this, whether it's tonight or tomorrow night or whenever – the next time, this is what we do. I'll distract him if he comes to me first, then we swap boxes.'

'What?'

'We swap boxes,' Molly repeated quietly, grinning broadly. 'If he fails any off the top, we've got him. D'you see?' Molly sat back, a look of triumph spread across her dainty features, her Irish eyes twinkling more than usual.

'He'll notice,' I protested.

'If we're quick while I distract him, they all look the same. He'll be failing pieces that he's just passed.'

'Gotcha,' whispered Madge.

'C'mon, Jean,' urged Molly. 'Are you game? We get him off your back and prove he's a liar at the same time.'

I felt nervous, unsure if I could pull it off.

'C'mon, Jean,' chorused the others quietly. 'You deserve justice.'

'You don't need to do anything,' said Molly. 'I'll make the swap. Leave it to me. All you have to do is work on as normal. You're one of my girls. We'll put a stop to this. You're losing money because of him.'

I felt nervous after the dinner break, but soon regained my rhythm at my lathe.

I hardly noticed Jack Harper at Molly's lathe. When he had finished inspecting Molly's sample, he slipped his micrometer into the top pocket of his cow gown.[17]

Lil working on the lathe to Molly's left called Jack over.

A distraction.

Molly quickly swapped her box with mine.

Jack Harper moved from Lil's lathe to mine, took his micrometer from his top pocket and measured a bolt from the top of the box. He shook his head as he

---

[17] A works overall in the style of a coat.

placed the 'offending' bolt on the bed of my lathe. These were soon joined by two more of Molly's pieces.

Molly left her lathe running, grabbed the three bolts and waved then in Harper's face.

'These have just been passed, by you!' she shouted, almost audible above the din of the shop. 'Switch off, Jean. Bring your box. We're going to the foreman's office.'

Molly switched off her lathe, picked up my box and headed for the stairs at the end of the shop. I didn't see the expression of Jack Harper's face. Several women watched us mount the steel steps to Dennis Collins's office.

Molly knocked, didn't wait for an answer, and bustled into the office, a torrent of complaints tumbling out of her mouth.

'Slow down, Miss O'Connor. Slow down, please,' pleaded the night foreman as he stood behind his desk, poised with a pencil in his hand. 'Let's all sit down, shall we.'

Molly recounted the whole incident, including the ones that led up to it.

Dennis Collins listened until Molly had finished, his grave expression indicating his concern.

'Here's the three. Would you check these first please,' she added.

'What's the job number?'

He looked up the number that Molly gave him in a bulky folder that lay on one side of his vast desk. A shiny micrometer lay amongst his pens and pencils.

The foreman measured the three failed bolts twice, nodding wordlessly.

'Is this your box, Miss Muir?'

'Yes.'

'My box has a tiny nick along one side,' added Molly.

Dennis Collins measured a sample from both boxes. 'I'll hang on to these,' he said. 'It's evidence. I'll send someone down with new boxes.'

'Okay, what happens now, Mr Collins? Jean has only been with us for a few weeks. I know she is a good worker. For a start, I taught her. She's been victimised, that's what.'

'It appears to be so. I will have to interview Jack, of course. You understand that I have to hear his side of what you are alleging.'

'Alleging! You've got the proof. He deliberately—'

'Calm down, Molly. I know what he did. I have to talk to him though. You must understand that.'

'Okay, I see. In the meantime, please make sure that this inspector does not come anywhere near Jean, me or any of my girls. You know who we are and where we are.'

'I do.'

'We'll continue to work hard for this firm, for you, and for the war effort. But keep that man out of our path.'

'Consider it done, Molly. It's almost tea break. If you go across now, you can grab an extra few minutes. Oh, and thank you for bringing this to my attention. You did the right thing.'

'Molly, Miss Muir,' he said as held the door of his office open.

The girls couldn't stop talking about it at tea break. Expressions of glee repeated over and over again rippled around our table until our cups of tea grew cold.

'He made him test the bolts in front of him,' said Lil excitedly at dinner break the next night.

'How do you know?' I asked.

'Lil has inside knowledge,' said Molly.

I listened while the girls exchanged what they knew or, perhaps, what they thought they knew, longing for the repercussions of the incident to be over. Molly had stood by me; of course, I was very grateful for that, but I felt self-conscious in an unfamiliar role as the centre of this kind of attention, longing to return to the routine of the machine shop as one of Molly's girls.

At the end of the shift the following night, Molly took me to one side after we had all changed out of our work clothes in the locker room.

'He's lost his job, Jean. I thought that you should know,' said Molly quietly, as if she only wanted me to hear.

I sat heavily on the bench, unable to reply.

It's my fault.

'I know what you're thinking, Jean. It isn't. Mr Collins told me. He called me into his office after dinner. They had no alternative. They have exacting standards here. It was wrong what Harper did. He didn't deny it to Collins. He had to be sacked, Jean. Think no more of it. There'll just be Arthur plus a new bloke, I suppose. They'll probably move someone from days. They've done that before now.'

I listened to Molly's explanation, all the while feeling my throat tighten and my breath shorten.

Molly sat next to me. Her tiny hand stopped mine from wringing and twisting.

'It's alright, Jean. It's over. C'mon, time to go home. Get some sleep. See you tonight.'

'Thanks, Molly. You are so kind,' I spluttered.

'I'm here to look after my girls. There's Madge. We'll be off.'

'You'll be alright, Jean,' said Madge on our way to the factory gate. 'We stick together to survive, eh.'

'Right enough,' I replied. 'See you tonight.'

Chapter Eight

A Summer of Bombs

Everyone at the factory had told me that the Birmingham Blitz had been at its worst before I joined the factory in May 1941. Even so, bombing raids at night continued sporadically throughout the summer of my first year as a factory worker. We always had half an eye on the large lamp above the clocking-in board, fearful of a red.

During my first few months, the blue lamp indicated that Birmingham was under attack on several occasions from the air. At the end of a blue shift, the locker room was not as noisy as usual. We were wary of what we might find as we made our way home.

We didn't see a red that summer. We worked through every blue light, even when raids were said to be heavy.

One morning towards the end of July, I walked home reflecting on my first three months of factory work. I had become an accomplished lathe operator according to Molly and Dennis Collins. I earned good money, saving some each month in the firm's saving scheme and sending a postal order home to Ma immediately after pay-day at the end of every week. It made me feel happy to contribute to housekeeping back home.

Although the work required a high level of concentration in a very noisy machine shop, I felt proud to be contributing to the war effort.

The grinding routine of twelve-hour shifts, six nights a week, left little time for anything else. I still went to the monthly dance; a few of the younger men proved bold enough to ask me to dance. My apparent reputation hadn't put them off. Some of the chaps were quite good dancers.

I didn't suffer from any more unwanted attention from any of the men.

Amidst the relentless routine, broken by the opportunity to let my hair down at the dances, I soon began to feel homesick. A nagging ache that started in the pit of my belly and worked its way upwards often came over me as I neared my digs, my temporary home.

An image of Fechan High Street was never far from my mind's eye. That morning in July was no exception.

What's going on?

I hurried up the hill towards my digs; the street a scene of chaos. The front of two terraces opposite Mrs Ellsworth's lay in a huge heap on the road. Firemen, ARP wardens and neighbours milled about.

'Keep back,' yelled an ARP warden.

Mrs Ellsworth stood on the pavement outside our front door.

'What's happened?' I asked, out of breath.

'I'd have thought that's pretty obvious, love,' said someone standing nearby.

The voice belonged to Mrs Thorpe, a well-known busybody and all round grumpy sole occupant of the terrace a few doors down.

'Why doesn't he stick to bombing you lot up at the factories?' she continued. 'I bet you've got proper shelters an' all, I'll be bound.'

'I wouldn't know. We work through the air raids,' I replied.

'Oh …'

'That's hardly fair, Ethel,' added my landlady. 'Jean's only doing her job.'

'Well …'

Mrs Ellsworth gestured for me to come inside.

'Miserable old bat,' she muttered as she banged the kettle down. 'Take no notice, Jean. I can see you're upset.'

'What happened?'

'The whole family were in the Anderson. They didn't stand a chance. Two stray bombs fell. One hit the roof and another exploded in the garden. The whole family … all three of them.'

'Is the father away?'

Mrs Ellsworth nodded.

'I can't imagine …'

'I know, Jean. It's awful. First direct hit on our street. Too close for comfort.'

'We knew there was a raid last night. Not where though,' I said.

My earlier feeling of pride in my working life, mingled with a regular sense of homesickness, was now touched with grief and guilt, guilt born out of the knowledge that our nearby factory and those around it are targets.

'I can imagine what you're thinking, Jean,' said my landlady. 'It's not your fault. There's always stray bombs. You've seen the ruined shops up the High Street. What've they got to do with the war? Nothing. That's what. We're all targets in this city,' Mrs Ellsworth added distractedly.

Not my fault, again.

'You sit there, Jean. I'll get breakfast ready.'

The only raid that sent us to the shelters occurred on the first Sunday in August, between tea break and dinner time. It took us a while to realise what was happening, so used were we to working through blue raids.

Molly tugged at my sleeve. 'Switch off, Jean,' she mouthed, pointing at the red lamp over the clock.

We barely heard the hooter signal over the usual din of the shop. Its sound registered as women switched off their lathes.

'Where do we go?' I mouthed.

'Follow us, Jean,' mouthed Molly.

I might have guessed. They've done this before.

I followed Molly and the others out of the machine shop into the yard. I looked skywards instinctively. Long shafts of white light from a myriad of searchlights slowly panned across the sky, searching for the bombers that we could hear but not see, an invisible threat that I heard for the first time since I came to Birmingham.

'C'mon, Jean,' urged Molly.

An ARP warden stood at the head of a flight of steps to the cellars below the canteen block; others were on the roof of the machine shop manning mobile water pumps. Instead of being in darkness, the roof of the building glowed with incendiaries, flickering wildly until they vanished, snuffed out one by one like a vicar quenching candles.

The sight of silhouettes of men moving amongst danger, amidst dozens of fires blazing around their feet, fixed me to the spot.

'Jean! This way,' urged Molly once more.

The persistence of Molly's instruction shook me out of my apparent trance. I followed the girls down a long flight of stone steps in almost complete darkness, only able to see faintly as the flicker of yellow candlelight greeted us as we neared the foot of the steps.

'Sorry, Molly,' I said. 'I've never experienced a raid before.'

'I know,' she replied.

'The roof is on fire,' I said, realising quickly that I had stated the obvious.

'The lads'll put 'em out quick,' said Lil. 'The fires don't do much damage. They're meant to show the bombers where to aim.'

'No direct hit yet this time,' said Peggy.

'Has the shop ever been hit?' I asked.

'Not yet, touch wood,' replied Molly, tapping the top of her black curls.

Wooden benches lined the walls of the huge cellar, providing enough room for all the workers to sit and wait for the all-clear.

'It's been a while since we had to sit in here,' said Madge. 'Thank goodness it's not too chilly.'

Down here you don't know what's going on outside.

Faces flickered in and out of focus in the gloom of the soft candlelight. Voices faded to whispers as if our conversations could be heard by the bombers, then dwindled until the cellar held its silent occupants in a patient vigil until the danger passed.

Molly placed a kindly hand on mine, calming their wringing and twisting. This time, my contorting hands reflected a different kind of anguish: fear, fear for myself, the girls, our street – a wave of fright shuddered through me. I held myself as still as I could. I didn't want to let the girls see that I was thoroughly terrified.

Molly squeezed gently. 'It's alright, Jean,' she whispered. 'We've all felt it. You'll get used to it.'

I attempted a weak smile. 'I'm okay, Molly. It's just the shock of seeing and hearing what we usually work through. A bomb killed a family opposite us a couple of weeks ago. It's just the unknown, not knowing what's going on up top.'

'I know,' said Molly. 'I heard about the family. These Andersons are feckin useless.'

Must be the Irish version.

Molly's profanity, or what I assumed to be a rude word, made us all giggle, breaking the quiet of our bomb shelter.

'Feck off, Adolf,' muttered Molly. 'We've got work to do.'

As if on cue, an ARP warden appeared at the foot of the steps. 'All clear ladies,' he announced to a chorus of groans and protestations.

'You've interrupted a good sit down,' came a voice from the gloom.'

'I was having a nice kip, Stan,' came another.

'C'mon ladies. I've heard it all before. Time to get back to it. Sorry, I'm only – '

'Doing my job,' chorused the reply.

We were met at the door to the cellar by our foreman. 'Go straight to dinner break, ladies,' he told us as we emerged into the yard.

I looked about me: everything looked undamaged as far as I could tell from the light of the moon bathing our place of work in a pale light.

The sky was silent, devoid of the bombers and searchlights. With Molly's girls around me, I didn't feel frightened for what was left of the night's shift.

Three more red alerts sent us scurrying to the shelter in August and September. Working through an air raid was no different from any other night shift, apart from noticing the light over the clock change from white to blue and back to white when the all-clear sounded across the city. We worked on, oblivious to what was happening outside.

Red alerts affected all of us, frightening and fearful in equal measure. From the apparent safety of the cellar, we could hear the bombers faintly and we could hear explosions as their deadly loads fell on the factory zone.

The raid in the second week of September created more noise than ever, rendering conversation in the cellar to almost nothing. I could not stop worrying what would happen if the building above us took a direct hit. Would we be buried alive under the rubble? How long before we were rescued?

Returning to the machine shop came as a blessed relief. I felt a strange sense of safety there, its racket insulating us from the consequences of yet another raid.

And it was worse before I started here.

It was only when I set off for my digs that I became aware of the damage caused by a red alert raid. Factories nearby lost buildings, while ours seemed untouched and invincible.

Will our luck hold out?

Shopkeepers sweeping broken glass became a familiar sight during the summer and autumn of 1941. Piles of rubble from destroyed business premises and houses near the factory zone often lay for days before its removal. At least damage to houses was less in evidence the further away from work the walk to my digs took me.

Perhaps I'm destined to be protected? I vowed to renew my prayers, asking for protection for Molly, her girls, and my landlady. Anyone missing from my list would be catered for by others doing their praying. If God listened to my modest list, then perhaps we'll survive the year.

*

Very few air raids occurred on Saturday nights during my first year as a factory worker. On such occasions, Mrs Ellsworth and I repaired to the Anderson shelter that her husband had erected in the back garden before he went to sea.

Our unspoken thoughts always turned to the tragedy that befell the family across the road as we sat in the damp shelter. We had no choice but to follow official advice and wait in the Anderson often for several hours until the all-clear sounded. We usually emerged at dawn and went directly to bed.

A particularly heavy raid took place in late September after a Saturday night dance. I was half-way home when sirens blasted out their warnings across the city. ARP wardens scurried about, barking orders for people to take cover.

'Where're you off to?' barked one from the other side of the street. I could barely see him without any street lighting.

'Home,' I shouted back.

'Get a move on then,' he called out. 'It's too dangerous to be out.'

'It's just around the corner,' I shouted.

I didn't wait for his reply and quickened my pace. I had done this walk dozens of times. I could do it in my sleep; I certainly could do it in the dark.

There seemed to be more searchlights than I had witnessed in past raids. Their bright white beams scanned back and forth, trying to pick out the bombers droning invisibly, their incessant roar unhindered by the thump of guns hurling shells into the night sky.

So this is what a big raid looks like.

Unwilling to encounter the wrath of any more ARP wardens, I hurried to my digs, let myself in to the darkened house and joined Mrs Ellsworth in the Anderson.

'I've been worried about you, Jean,' she said with a sigh.

'I'm okay, thank you,' I replied. 'This is a big one. It started just as we left the dance.'

'I've made a flask of tea. Would you like one?'

'Ooh, yes please.'

'I've only the one cup,' she added.

We sat in the dark as we had done on many occasions since I came to live with her, waiting for the fear to pass, listening for explosions, judging their distance. Thin light seeping into the Anderson coincided with the sound of the all-clear.

'That's another one over, Jean. We can go in now.'

I can't say I got used to it. Every raid was frightening. All I knew was I had to get on with it; this was my duty. Getting used to being under attack was something we had to do. They didn't tell us anything about such things when I was conscripted.

Raids continued sporadically, punctuating the routine of week after week of night shifts. My first summer of bombs turned into autumn; the winter of 1941 beckoned without any sign of leave. Homesickness abated to some extent, replaced by fear of being bombed at my digs or at work, only to return as my first Christmas away from home approached.

Concentrating on accurate work at my lathe served to dampen my anxiety. Working through all but the raids that threatened the machine shop was a godsend. I could almost forget what might be happening outside when the lamp showed blue. As December wore on, thoughts of home had a habit of breaking through my concentration, forcing silent feelings to the surface at break times.

'Penny for 'em,' said Lil, at dinner break the Monday before Christmas.

'I diagnose homesickness. Am I right, Jean?' said Molly.

'Just a bit,' I replied. 'I've been away from home for almost eight months now, the longest ever. Do we get any time off over Christmas?'

'Not much. A day usually,' said Lil.

'Oh well, I can wait. It's not worth getting the train to Scotland just for one day. I'd have to come back just as soon as I arrive.'

I'll write Ma and send a PO.

And so, my summer of bombs receded. The winter of 1941 loomed like a dark cloud with no prospect of a visit home.

Word spread that those who wanted to work on the Thursday and Friday of that week, Christmas Day and Boxing Day, would be rewarded with a higher piece rate than normal. I volunteered to work over the Christmas period, hoping that some leave would come my way once I had completed my first year of war work.

An incident in the machine shop during the night shift before Christmas Eve brought forward leave in a most unexpected way.

As I returned from a toilet break, I heard a scream near the exit from the ladies' lavatory.

A young woman working on a lathe at the opposite end of the shop from Molly's girls screeched wildly, her head bent alarmingly near the chuck of her lathe.

Her neighbour hit the stop button; I grabbed the nearest piece of rag I could see and gripped the chuck with all my might.

'She's got her hair caught,' I mouthed as loudly as I could, although it must have been obvious to those gathered round what had happened.

Blood seeped out of the woman's scalp and trickled down her face, forming red globules on the surface of the end of her lathe.

I gripped harder, to stop the chuck pulling at what was left of her hair on the left side of her head.

'Keep still,' yelled someone. 'Stop pulling.'

The stricken woman finally stopped trying to jerk herself free. A pair of scissors appeared magically, and she was cut loose.

The woman fell back in a dead faint into the arms of one of the setters.

A large crowd gathered around the scene of the incident. 'Let me pass,' indicated the setter, lifting the woman. 'Someone go ahead and tell the FAP.'

'Are you alright, love?' mouthed an elderly machinist.

I looked at my hands, redness spreading rapidly across both palms.

'You'd better get that seen to,' said another woman pointing at my hands. 'I've told her before about her turban.'

'You were very brave,' mouthed the elderly machinist. 'It could have been far worse but for you.'

'What's been going on down there, Jean,' mouthed Molly when I got back to my lathe. 'I thought I heard a scream.'

'You did,' I mouthed, recounting the incident.

'Let's have a look,' mouthed Molly.

'Blimey, Jean. You mustn't carry on with your hands like this. You'll have to take some time off. Get yourself to FAP. I'll send for Mr Collins. No buts. Get yourself along there now.'

I sat next to the injured machinist in FAP. Her head was swathed in a large dressing.

'How are you feeling?' I asked.

'It's very painful. It could have been much worse. Someone stopped my chuck.'

'An ambulance is on its way, Maureen,' said the nurse. 'It was this lady here.'

'Really … oh, thank you … thank you. Oh, your poor hands.'

'I'll take you down, Maureen,' said the nurse. 'I'll be back shortly, Miss Muir.'

Maureen paused at the door, turned and said: 'I can't thank you enough.'

'Take care now,' I replied.

The nurse gave me a large tub of ointment. 'Rub on gently three times a day,' she instructed.

'I sleep during the day.'

'Of course. Well, when you can then. This'll take the sting out. I've seen worse. It'll take a few days. You'll live.'

The nurse also gave me a pair of silk gloves. 'After you've rubbed in the ointment, wear these at all times. Your skin with itch for a while until your palms heal.'

'Can I operate my lathe wearing these?"

'No. I'll recommend a few days rest from work to Mr Collins.'

'Oh, I see.'

I'll lose money.

'How do your hands feel?'

'A bit sore. Hot and stingy.'

'Well, you mustn't work for a while.'

'Is Maureen badly injured? It looked awful.'

'It looked worse than it is, if you see what I mean. What you did saved her skin from contacting the chuck. Ah, Mr Collins.'

'Would you come to my office when you're ready, Miss Muir,' he said.

'Okay, Jean, you're done,' said the nurse.

'Thank you, nurse,' I said.

Mr Collins gestured to me to take a seat in front of his untidy desk.

'Thank you for what you did. Your quick thinking saved a worse situation. In all my time here, I've seen only two incidents of hair caught in machinery. I'll be issuing reminder notices about the careful use of hair covering,' he added distractedly, as if to himself.

'Right, Miss Muir,' he announced, leaning back in his chair, both palms flat on his desktop. 'Tomorrow is Christmas Eve. I note that you haven't had any leave yet. Do you need help with train fare?'

'Er, no. I've plenty saved.'

'I would like you to have a few days off. You need time for your hands to heal.'

'I'll miss the extra money over Christmas,' I said.

'Well, never mind about that. You can't operate your lathe just yet. Will you go home to Scotland?'

'Yes, if there's a train tomorrow. Later today, I mean.'

'Good. You are a very good worker, Miss Muir. Molly talks highly of you. I need you back here fit and well.'

'Thank you, Mr Collins. Molly taught me well.'

'Very good. This is what I propose. Here's your wages for this week, made up with a basic for the nights you won't be working.'

Mr Collins handed me one of the usual brown envelopes sealed at one end.

'It's almost dinner time,' he said, glancing at the large clock on the wall above his office door. 'Go on your dinner break now, then go home and get some sleep. I've got a timetable somewhere. I'll look up trains: to where exactly?'

'Carlisle.'

'Carlisle. I'll send a message to the canteen. Despite the military, the timetable still seems to operate more or less as printed. I'll send James to tidy up your lathe.'

'This is very generous of you, Mr Collins,' I said, holding up the envelope.

'Until Sunday the fourth of January then,' he said, smiling broadly. 'Look after those hands. We need 'em.'

Mr Collins stood and held out his right hand. 'Oh, sorry, better not.'

A ripple of applause greeted me at the dinner table.

'She's gone as red as her poor hands,' quipped Peggy.

'Well done, Jean,' chorused Molly's girls.

My liver, bacon, mash, and peas were almost cold by the time I answered everyone's questions.

I parted company with the girls on my way to the locker room to get changed.

'We'll miss you, Jean,' said Molly.

'Are you working over Christmas?' I asked her.

'No. I don't mind a short week's pay. At least it's voluntary on Thursday and Friday. Last year it wasn't. I'm back in on Sunday. Have a lovely time at home and look after those hands.'

Molly squeezed my elbow and disappeared across the yard in the gloom.

I opened the front door of my digs as quietly as I could. Mrs Ellsworth would not be expecting me at this hour of the night.

Sleep eventually overcame the anticipation of a home visit, mingled with a ceaseless tingling in my right hand. I tried to remember how I had grabbed Maureen's chuck. One hand on top, one hand under is how I think I managed it.

I would have some explaining to do to the folks back home.

Chapter Nine

Home is Another Country

I had expected to work my normal shifts during the Christmas period. Mrs Ellsworth had told me that she would be spending Christmas with her sister in Worcester and worried that I would be on my own while she was away. She was relieved that I had leave to go home, but worried even more when she saw the state of my injuries.

The nurse had given me a spare pair of white silk gloves before I had left work last night: 'So you always have a clean pair' she had advised. 'Take them off at night after you've used the ointment.'

It was rather painful taking the gloves off and putting them back on. I kept them on during the train journey.

The regular pulsing in the thumb in my right hand had almost faded by the time the train reached Carlisle. Perhaps the healing process had begun to work.

Arriving sleepily at Carlisle railway station in the afternoon of Christmas Eve 1941 contrasted sharply with the beginning of my train journey earlier that day. The streets of Carlisle were devoid of piles of rubble; shopkeepers weren't sweeping up broken glass and nowhere was boarded up. Carlisle looked and felt as if the war didn't exist up here, far to the north of the bombers' targets in the Midlands. I felt the ever-present sense of fear of being bombed lift as I mingled with Christmas Eve shoppers thronging the streets near the station.

They have no idea.

I had time to make some purchases before catching the last bus of the afternoon to the Fechan: a small bottle of sherry for Ma; pipe tobacco for Pa; a Christmas Cake for Aunty Chrissie; toy soldiers and aeroplanes for my three youngest brothers, woolly socks for my brother William, and a colourful purse for my sister Betty. I didn't know whether my sisters Danny or Kathy would be home from their war work, so I rounded off my shopping with a tin of sweets and a tin of Scottish shortbread for the family to share. The presents went into a canvas bag that I had borrowed from Mrs Ellsworth.

I went over what I was going to give to whom for the umpteenth time when the Broon Moor came into view on the left-hand side of the bus as it rattled its way towards the village.[18] My chest thudded as the familiar sight of this distinctive landmark told me that I was almost there, nearly home, somewhere I could feel safe from the war that rained down on us in Birmingham.

I gazed at the peaceful rows of terraced houses as the bus pulled into Ecclefechan High Street before it continued its route to Lockerbie.

I was the only passenger to alight at the bus stop by the corner shop. I stood for a moment after the noisy bus had vanished out of earshot, revelling in the peace and quiet of the sleepy street. The noise of the machine shop ceased its echo in my head: Ecclefechan was smothered in silence in the falling dusk.

The shock of familiarity, the very *sameness* divorced from the reality of war gladdened me; I felt light-

---

[18] The Brown Moor (locally known as the Broon Moor) is a high, wooded moor just to the west of the southerly approach to Ecclefechan.

headed. The intervening months since my departure in May seemed to evaporate, as if I had left yesterday and returned a day later.

I picked up my bags and started along the street to Aunty Chrissie's terrace.

There'll be lots of questions, I'll be bound, most of which I won't be permitted to answer.

Repeated instructions to maintain silence about our work troubled me when I knocked on my aunty's door.

'What're ee dain hame?' she exclaimed.

'I had no time to write,' I explained. 'I was only granted leave yesterday.'

'Come away in, Jean. It's grand tae see ee. Danny's here. She's up at yer Ma's. Kathy's no here though.'

'I'll away up and see Ma and Pa before I settle in if that's alright. I can stay, can't I?'

'Of course ee can. See ee in a wee while.'

'This is for you,' I said, finding the Christmas cake in my bag of gifts.

'Thanks, Jean. Ah havenae made yin this year. Ye'll be sharing with Danny in the spare room. A'reet.'

'Aye. Ah'll be back shortly,' I replied.

'Ee havenae completely lost yer accent doon there amongst the English.'

'Ah feel it coming back now Ah'm hame,' I said.

'There ee are, then,' said Chrissie.

The front door to Ma and Pa's terrace was ajar, despite the chill of the December evening.

'Hello,' I called out as I pushed the door open and stepped inside.

A fire blazed in the grate, warming the tiny downstairs room. Ma kneaded dough and Danny darned a sock. There was no sign of the younger bairns.

My mother and my sister stopped what they were doing: hugs, kisses, and a stream of questions directed at me almost knocked me off my feet.

'Let me get ma breath back,' I pleaded.

Danny understood why I couldn't say much about my war work: she didn't say much about what she was doing either.

'Ah work in a noisy factory, Ma,' I explained. 'All night.'

'A' neet!' she exclaimed.

'Aye, ee get used til it,' I said, hearing my Fechan accent seep into my speech. 'How's Pa?'

'He's a'reet,' replied my mother. 'He gets bits and pieces of work here and there. There's nae much tae be had. Yer postal orders are a great help, Jeanie.'

'Aye, well, Ah'm glad of that,' I said.

I searched in my handbag for an envelope and handed it to my mother.

'Ah'll give ee this now, afore Pa gets hame,' I said.

My mother peeped inside the envelope. 'A' this,' she said.

'Dinnae let on how much Ah've given ee. Use it as and when ee want.'

My mother went upstairs with the envelope.

'Ah hope ee dinnae min,' I said to Danny.[19]

'Course not. Ah've given her some money just now. She needs it.'

'It's grand to see ee baith,' said Ma, returning to her kneading. 'Ah've missed ee a'. Davie cannae be hame of course. Neither can Kathy.'

---

[19] Jean and her sister, Danny, often spoke to one another in the Fechan accent when they were in Birmingham or Ecclefechan.

'Aye, we'll hae a family gathering,' said Danny. 'As many Muirs as we can muster.'

'Here's Pa.'

My father closed the front door behind him, beamed with delight and laid a large sack on the kitchen table. 'Two chickens in there for ee, Kate,' he announced proudly. 'It's aye grand tae see ee baith.'

The same questions from my father met with our stock replies.

'We're under strict instructions,' said Danny.

My father nodded, reluctantly accepting our vague explanations as he hung his thick work jacket over the back of one of the kitchen chairs.

'Ah've made a scone,' announced Danny.

My father rubbed his hands together and sat at the table.

'Ah'll just set this tae prove,' said my mother, 'and butter ee yin o' Danny's scones.'

'Aye, the Muirs can mak a scone,' said Pa. 'Even Ah can. Yours are better though,' he said to Ma and then to Danny. 'It's grand tae hae some o' ma eldest hame.'

My father suddenly noticed my gloved hands.

I told them as much as I dared about the incident. 'That's why Ah'm on leave,' I explained, taking my gloves off.

Ma and Pa examined my hands gingerly.

'Does it hurt?' asked Danny.

'A little,' I replied. 'They're healing already.'

'Onyway, at least they sent ee hame,' said Ma. 'Time tae heal properly.'

I carefully drew my gloves on, glad that the friendly inquisition was over.

*

The next few days amongst family brought on a sense of unease. I found the stark contrast between the fellowship of family and the camaraderie of Molly's girls a struggle to come to terms with. Feeling homesick had been assuaged to an extent, replaced by an unexpected and unrealistic reluctance to return to doing my duty. I took to taking long walks near the village in an attempt to purge my fear of being bombed.

Danny noticed my periods of silence while we sat at table in Aunty Chrissie's terrace. 'Penny for 'em, Jean.'

I sighed, cupped my chin in my hands and faced my sister.

'Aye, Ah know. The war disnae impinge on them up here, does it?' she said.

'That's a good thing though, isn't it?' I replied.

'They dinnae ken whit's garn on,' said Danny. 'They dinnae read a national paper, so how can they know what it's like.'

'Best if the Fechan is insulated from it all,' I suggested. 'Gives us a haven of peace.'

'When will ee next get leave?' asked Danny.

'Next summer, Ah believe,' I said. 'You?'

'Ah dinnae ken. We're lucky tae be able tae come back here. C'mon, we've tae be away up the road tae help wi denner.'

New Year's Eve dinner was a two-sitting affair, just as Christmas dinner had been: one sitting at mid-day for our younger brothers and sister, and one in the evening for Ma, Pa, Danny, Marion, Aunty Chrissie, and me.

Ma cooked the chickens on Christmas morning; our Hogmanay dinner comprised a large pot of stewed vegetables and mutton that she purchased with some of the money I gave her.[20]

Aunty Chrissie surprised us with a bottle of single malt after dinner, rounding off a splendid Hogmanay family feast. 'Whi's fi first footin'?' she announced.[21]

'You youngsters should go,' said Ma. 'We'll see in the New Year here.'

Marion, me, and Danny – the one, three, and five of the ten Muir siblings – spent the next hour or so wandering along the High Street first footing until I began to feel decidedly groggy.

'That's enough whisky,' I mumbled when we came out of Number 10.

'Aye, me too,' said Marion. 'Ah'm away tae ma bed. Happy New Year.'

'Happy New Year,' we chorused.

Arm in arm, Danny and me stumbled to Aunty Chrissie's terrace, yearning for our beds too, longing for Ecclefechan to stop spinning beneath our feet.

'Ah wonder whit nineteen forty-two will bring,' I said quietly as I pulled the covers to my chin, shivering in my aunty's spare bedroom.

My sister didn't reply. Danny breathing loudly next to me hadn't heard me.

---

[20] Hogmanay is the Scottish word for the last day of the old year and is synonymous with the celebration of the New Year in the Scottish manner, including first-footing,

[21] which refers to the first person to enter a household on New Year's Day, seen as a bringer of good luck for the year to come.

Chapter Ten

"When sorrows come ... "
Hamlet Act IV, Scene V

I returned to Birmingham the day following New Year's Day in time for the first shift of the new year on the Sunday.

Tearful farewells played out in my mind during spells of dreamily gazing out of the window during the train journey from Carlisle. Us sisters didn't know when we would see one another again or when next we would see Ma and Pa.

'Look efter yersel, Jean,' said Pa. 'Ah'm away tae ma work afore ee garn.'

'Aye. Ah'll let ee know when Ah'm coming next time,' I said.

'Dinnae get grabbing ony mair machinery,' he added, smiling briefly before he closed the front door behind him.

The lump in my throat returned as I recalled parting from Ma and Pa earlier that day.

Duty calls, duty calls.

This overriding thought accompanied my return to Birmingham at the end of my period of unexpected leave. I hadn't wanted to leave home but kept this to myself. I suspect that Danny read my thoughts as we sat without saying much to one another for most of the bus journey from Ecclefechan to Carlisle.

'Ma'll be a'reet. Dinnae ee fret,' said Danny while we waited at Carlisle railway station. 'That's me, Jean,' she added quickly as her train was announced.

110

'Take care, Danny,' I whispered in her ear as we hugged.

'You too,' she replied, still holding me for a few moments.

I watched my younger sister walk across the station's concourse, hoping for a final wave. One came as she turned before disappearing into the throng of travellers moving towards her platform.

My thoughts and daydreams were full of home as we approached Birmingham. Now that I had tasted home, I was not looking forward to the shop floor.

It's got to be done though.

Opening the front door and hearing my landlady's cheery welcome made me feel happier about the prospect of returning to war work and the constant threat of bombs.

Mrs Ellsworth didn't quiz me about my enforced leave. Somehow she detected my low spirits, cleverly avoiding the subject by telling me about Christmas with her sister and family.

I listened to her story, glad to hear about her time away without having to tell her about mine.

'When do you start back, Jean?' she asked at length.

'Tomorrow night,' I replied.

'And your hands, are you well enough to operate your machine?'

'Very much better, thank you,' I replied.

'It's a wonder they don't provide gloves,' Mrs Ellsworth added, clearing away the teacups. 'Why couldn't you wear special gloves?'

'No one does,' I said. 'I don't know what would be suitable.'

'Humph,' muttered Mrs Ellsworth. 'It's not good enough,' she added, as if talking to herself.

*

My first Sunday night shift of the New Year proved uneventful. I soon regained the routine, starting slowly, making sure that my hands were as nimble as before.

'Let me see,' demanded Molly at the first break. She examined my palms, turning them over in her tiny hands. 'Hmm, they look a lot better. Pop into the FAP at dinner time; see what she says.'

The nurse pronounced me fit to work and provided me with some more silk gloves and another tub of ointment. The injury hadn't interfered with my work; by the time I walked home in the dark on Monday morning, I felt confident enough to face the coming weeks and months of my conscription.

I tried to put thoughts of leave aside as I made my way along darkened streets, where the absence of dawn concealed any evidence of the night's bombing.

As far as I could tell, it had been a quiet night. Firemen and ARP wardens thankfully absent along the route to my digs.

I told myself that I would buckle down and survive, get through the war however long it took and come out the other side.

I let myself in and went directly to bed.

I heard crying in a dream, realistic and alarming enough to jolt me awake. For a moment I didn't know where I was, until the bedroom ceiling came into focus and the final scene of the dream eluded my memory.

I could still hear crying though; it seemed more distant than in my dream. I sat up in bed, confused, listening, trying to make sense of what I could hear.

The unmistakable sound of weeping got louder as I inched open the bedroom door. I put on my dressing gown and slippers and descended the stairs slowly, dreading what I would find.

Mrs Ellsworth sat with her back to me at the kitchen table; she shook with sobs. Her hands, face down, clamped what appeared to be the source of her distress to the surface of the table, as if to trap its contents or deny its existence.

The likely content of the piece of paper leapt into my mind.

Oh no!

I froze for a moment, standing in the doorway of the kitchen, unsure what to do.

I was on the point of backing out of the door when Mrs Ellsworth turned, her sobs subsiding. The lump in my throat almost robbed me of speech.

'He's not coming back, Jean. Oh, Jean.'

Mrs Ellsworth handed me the piece of paper. I read it quickly. The official-looking letter told of the sinking of HMS Athena in the Atlantic Ocean. Ordinary Seaman Ellsworth was not amongst the known survivors.

I sat opposite my landlady, fighting back tears, thoughts of my brother Davie competing with news of her loss.

'It came this morning,' she said, her voice weak and tearful.

What a shock.

Words failed me; I reached across the table and placed my hands over hers, squeezing gently. After a few moments of silent eye contact, I found my voice.

'I am so sorry, Mrs Ellsworth. So very sorry.'

'Thank you, Jean. I must have been sitting here for ages. And I've woken you up.'

'Never mind that,' I said, getting to my feet. 'Have you had any breakfast?'

Mrs Ellsworth shook her head.

I busied myself making tea and toast, which gave me the opportunity to gently remove the letter from the table, fold it and put it on the sideboard.

'You ought not be on your own,' I said as I set out the breakfast things.

'I think I will go to my sister's for a while.'

'Good idea,' I replied.

'No time to write and tell her. I'll go this afternoon.'

'I'll go into town to the station with you,' I suggested.

'I'll be all right, Jean. You need to get some sleep before you go to work. Thank you anyway. I can trust you to look after the house while I'm away.'

'Of course.'

'I'll be gone by the time you get up. There's some ham in the fridge for a sandwich. You'll have to do some shopping for food while I'm away.'

'Don't you worry. I'll be fine,' I said. 'You just get yourself to your sister's. You should be amongst family.'

'Thank you, Jean. I'm so glad you were here when I got the news. At least I wasn't entirely alone. You ought to go back to bed now.'

It took me a long time to fall asleep. I wasn't sure if my thoughts of my family and my brother Davie at sea were just that: me thinking about him and the others, or whether my jumbled thoughts had turned into dreams. In any event, I must have dropped off because my alarm clock woke me with a start.

Mrs Ellsworth had left me a brief note on the kitchen table, giving me the address of her sister.

Oh good, I'll write to her soon.

I tried to imagine my landlady, sitting in the train to Worcester, nursing an unimaginable ache: the death of her husband.

I had never lost anyone; I couldn't imagine what it must feel like. Witnessing such grief earlier in the day was one thing, feeling it was something that might be visited upon me eventually.

An image of Ma and Pa reading a letter about one of us sprang into my mind. I pushed it away.

We'll survive this; we will.

I noticed that Lil wasn't at her lathe on Monday evening. I mouthed to Molly, asking where she was.

'I'll tell you at break time,' she mouthed back.

The girls were subdued at tea break. I feared more bad news.

'The bomber was shot down over Germany,' Molly announced quietly.

Silence and downcast faces met the news about Lil's son.

'He might have been captured,' suggested Peggy.

'Possible,' replied Molly. 'She won't know yet.'

'Do the Germans let the Government know who's been captured?' asked Madge.

'I think so. We'll just have to wait and see,' said Molly. 'In the meantime, Lil won't be coming in.'

More tragedy. Two in one day.

'You all right, Jean?' asked Molly.

'My landlady's man was lost at sea. She heard this morning. His ship was sunk in the Atlantic. And now this. I'm sorry,' I said, fishing for a handkerchief in the pocket of my overalls.

"S'alright, Jean,' said Molly.

'Don't feel sorry about upsetting yourself,' added Peggy. 'This bloody war is getting too close to home. Let's all pray for no more bad news of loved ones. Let's make more planes and finish off that bugger Hitler,' she added, banging her fist on the table, rattling cups and saucers.

No more was said after Peggy's outburst almost silenced the canteen. We put our tea things on the end of the counter and went back to work with a vengeance.

I made more bolts that night than during any previous shift. Was it anger that drove me to work faster, or was it something else? I didn't know.

Just before dinner break, I was rather short with Stan, our setter, when my lathe needed attention.

'Hold up, Jean,' he mouthed. 'I'm doing the best I can.'

'Sorry, Stan,' I mouthed. 'It was going so well tonight.'

Stan tinkered and adjusted until he was satisfied.

'There y'are, Jean,' he mouthed. 'Away you go.'

'Thanks, Stan,' I mouthed. 'I think Molly's has stopped.'

Stan moved along to see to Molly's lathe.

I added to my night's tally, every screw placed in my box with a message: *end it soon; no more missing men.*

The war didn't end that day or in the days and months that followed. Air raids continued to hurl their deadly cargo onto the city, all of which I was unaware of until I left the factory early in the dark mornings.

As the days lengthened, the bomb damage to nearby houses and factories revealed itself, no longer hidden by the darkness. I became so used to the sight of broken glass and rubble, I almost grew immune to its familiarity, barely wanting to think about the human cost that might lie beneath broken houses and wrecked buildings. I wondered just how much longer my factory would survive if the raids continued.

Perhaps it's just a matter of time before our luck runs out.

*

Our luck almost did run out on the night of Wednesday 29th July. Since the Monday of that week, Birmingham suffered particularly heavy air raids.

Half-way into our shift on the Wednesday, the red light over the clock signalled an end to work. Lathes slowed down and stopped, and we filed out of the building into a night lit up by dozens of incendiaries flaming on the roofs all around us. Flames and smoke leapt from the roof of the shop. Teams of men could be seen silhouetted against the smoke, frantically pumping water, generating steam hissing through the crackle of the fires of the incendiary bombs.

Cries of the men on the roof and the rumble of the bombers struck fear into me as we rushed across the yard and down the steps into the cellars.

'I've never seen so many incendiaries,' said Molly as we settled onto the wooden benches in the cellar.

'It'll be a miracle if the shop survives this one,' added Lil.

I glanced at Lil in admiration. Since the news of the death of her son when his bomber was shot down, she had come back to work; companionship had helped her to cope with her grief.

'I wish that he had been captured, Jean,' she had said to me at dinner break on her first night back. 'But there we are, it wasn't to be. I'm not the only one to lose someone.'

'The shop's lit up like a firework,' said Lil in the gloom of the cellar. 'We're a bloody sitting target.'

'Don't worry, girls,' said Molly. 'The lads'll put 'em out. Hitler'll have nothing to go at.'

It was almost light when we were given the all-clear. We stepped into the yard, fearing the worst.

Trails of smoke and whisps of steam rose from the roof of the shop: the building looked undamaged.

'Hooray,' chorused Molly's girls.

We live to fight another day.

Only an hour or so remained of that night's shift, so we were instructed to reckon up our piece work and leave our lathes ready for the day shift and go home early. While we were in the locker room, the news came through that one of the men would not live to fight another day. Stan, our lovely Stan, had lost his life as a result of his injuries. He had been on the roof of the shop when an incendiary exploded near where he was helping to put others out.

'I didn't know that he was on fire duty last night,' said Lil.

Nobody spoke while we changed out of our work clothes. Quiet "goodbyes" were exchanged as we left the building. The thought of Stan missing from the shop came at the end of an horrific night of bombing. The factory and us girls had come through it unscathed: Stan's family had not.

I walked slowly home, unable to stop thinking about Stan, his patience and skill as a setter unwavering even when we were anxious about our piece work earnings when our lathes broke down.

I wish I hadn't been cross with him.

The first few months of 1942 had seen the drudgery of factory work punctuated by tragedy. I hadn't known what to expect when I started work the year before, neither what factory work would be like, nor what an air raid would be like. The former was alien and the latter was reported only in general terms in the Carlisle newspaper. The only air raid in the Midlands that was fully reported took place in November 1940 in the city of Coventry, several months before I left home for Birmingham. The shock of seeing photographs of the ruined cathedral was dreadful, but I had no inkling that a year or so later I would be anywhere near anything remotely similar.

I told myself that I had grown up since leaving the doctor's employ in Carlisle. I had seen how tragedy and the loss of a loved one took its toll on my new friends. I had witnessed the brutal damage wreaked by German bombers and I had been in the midst of heavy air raids on our factory. I had survived a year of the war.

I also told myself that the air raids would continue and loss of life would continue. After the death of Stan, I felt conflicted between homesickness and the desire to carry on making my minor contribution to the war effort count.

"Let's make more planes," Lil had said.

Her words echoed in my mind as I began that Thursday night's shift, determined to get through without having to call Arthur over to fix my lathe. His workload would increase until a replacement could be found for Stan. If my lathe behaved, I planned to work faster than ever.

This one's for Stan.

I switched on, swung the turret and set the swarf flying. Completed bolts stacked up in my box for the next five and a half hours.

'Blimey, Jean,' said Molly at the dinner break. 'You saving up for something?'

'Ma needs my help with the young uns. Pa doesn't always find work. What with my brother at sea, it's up to my sisters and me to help support the family.'

'Well, don't overdo it,' said Molly. 'Mistakes can happen if you go too fast. We're all upset about Stan and Lil's boy. Being angry doesn't help.'

She's read my mind.

'Take it steady,' Molly whispered when we put our plates and cutlery on the counter.

'Aye, I will,' I replied.

Molly hooked her arm in mine as we followed the others out of the canteen. This simple act of kindness lifted my mood, reassured me that we would come through this together. Molly began as my teacher; now she looked out for me as one of her girls, protected by her like a mother and a friend to us all.

Chapter Eleven

The Invasion of Ecclefechan

They told us at the induction session on our first morning that we would be entitled to one week's holiday per year. Over a year elapsed by the time my week's holiday was granted in August 1942, a week after the massive air raid of the night of 29th July.

I worked my shifts until Friday 7th August, accumulating as much bonus pay as I could without drawing undue attention from Molly at the lathe next to me. I felt flush with cash as I said goodbye to the girls on Saturday morning, messages of "Have a lovely time" echoing in my ears as I walked quickly home.

'Are you sure you're okay going today?' asked Mrs Ellsworth.

'I'll have a few hours' sleep and catch this afternoon's train up,' I replied. 'I'm only away a week. Will you be all right on your own?'

'Don't you worry about me, Jean. You just enjoy yourself at home. You deserve a break.'

I caught a local train from Carlisle to Lockerbie instead of catching a bus to the Fechan. The short walk from Ecclefechan station to the village would, I decided, do me good. A walk past fields and farms close to familiar landmarks would be refreshing; the clear country air a longed-for change to dusty streets and bombed out buildings.

I was not disappointed.

I waited for the train to pull away in the direction of Lockerbie until I heard it no longer, leaving me standing alone on the platform. The peace and quiet almost came as a shock: all I could hear was birdsong and the distant sound of a tractor.

Could be on the Moran's farm.

I wondered if my mother or father had stood where I now stood during the First World War, before I was born on a journey home from somewhere, anxious and excited to be going home after a period of absence just like me. I also wondered if I should ask them one day.

As I approached the Fechan along the Lockerbie to Carlisle Road, I noticed that our sleepy village appeared to be surrounded by army vehicles.

'Whit's garn on, Aunty?' I said when Aunty Chrissie let me in.

'We've been invaded, Jean. Some numpty in the airmy picked on iss fi a mock invasion. They're a' camped ower yonder, at the foot of the Broon Moor.' My aunty clattered the tea things nosily, exaggerating her irritation. 'The actual invasion is on the moran's moran. There's a dance the night in the hall if ee're keen tae meet a soldier.'

A dance!

'Some o' the young lassies might be only too glad. Efter a', there's nae ony young men left in the village. Might ee garn?'

'Ah might just dae that. We have dances at the factory. There's a really good dance band. Not many young men though.'

After cups of tea and tatty scones, I helped my aunty clear away the tea things.

'Just yersel in the spare room this time,' she said. 'You're the only yin on leave.'

'Ah'll away up and see Ma and Pa just now,' I said.

'A'reet, Jean. They're looking forward tae seeing ee.'

Pa came in moments after I did. 'It's good tae see ee, Jean,' he said, giving me a brief hug, then holding me away from him in his work clothes.

'Working on a Saturday afternoon?' I said.

'Ah hae tae tak a' the work Ah can, Jean. It comes and goes.'

Ma set out teacups for the three of us.

'Where're the wee uns?' I asked.

'Oot playing,' replied Ma.

'Ah'll see 'em later, or tomorrow,' I said. 'By the way, whit's garn tae happen the day after tomorrow?'

'They'll enter the village in vehicles and pretend tae shoot down snipers,' replied Pa. 'Some soldiers wull be up on roofs and the like. We've been told tae stay indoors. There'll be blanks fired.'

'Ah'll be glad when it's a' ower,' muttered Ma.

'It's good practice, Kate,' said Pa. 'The Fechan is helping wi the war effort. Talking of which, thanks very much for the postal orders. They help a lot.'

'Aye, Jean, they help a lot,' added Ma.

'Ah'm earning good money as well as helping with the war,' I said.

'Birmingham and Ecclefechan: helping to beat Hitler,' said Pa, laughing and smiling.

The army provided a very fine dance band, playing a mixture of traditional ballroom dances and modern swing. I recognised a few faces from my school days amongst the groups of girls that sat nervously around the edge of an empty dancefloor. Equally nervous soldiers in their uniforms propped up the bar.

After a few slow numbers, the bandleader turned to face the room. 'C'mon gentlemen,' he called out. 'There are lots of lovely Scottish lassies waiting to be asked. So, put yer pints down and show 'em what the army is made of.'

Peals of laughter erupted from around the room.

'C'mon, men. Do your duty,' called the band leader.

A tall soldier, wearing a grin that spread from ear to ear was the first to stride across the room. He stopped in front of me, clicked his heels, bowed briefly and asked me to dance.

He led me to the centre of the dance floor and waited for the band.

'Thank you, Corporal Etheridge. Not afraid of the lassies then,' said the bandleader.

The band struck up a quickstep. Corporal Etheridge swept me around the dance floor as if we'd danced together before. We must have looked the part; the expert couple holding the floor, impressing the onlookers. Our dominance was, thankfully, short-lived; Corporal Etheridge's friends took courage from his first move. Soon the dance floor vibrated to the steps of couples swirling around, avoiding one another expertly.

The war that had been a distant reality on my previous visits home, far away from our sleepy village, now had come closer. Benign attacking forces would gather just as soon as the men stopped enjoying themselves with the womenfolk of their mock enemy.

At eleven o'clock on the day of the mock invasion, Ma, Pa, the boys, and me crowded around the window that faced the High Street, my younger brothers showing their excitement as heavy vehicles entered the village. This was followed by the clatter of boots on the road and pavement as several soldiers swept past the window.

At the sound of soldiers running along the street, Pa suddenly turned away and went out of the back door. I glanced at my mother. No sign of an explanation was forthcoming in her expression.

More soldiers ran past, followed by jeeps and covered trucks.

My brothers chattered excitedly, pointing and waving.

Then we heard gunfire.

'That's why we were told tae stay indoors,' I suggested.

'Hey, real gunfire,' shouted Hiddleston.

'Blanks,' corrected his older brother, William.

Murray covered his ears.

After twenty or thirty minutes of noise and activity along the High Street, a loud knock on our front door drew my attention away from the window.

'Ah'll get it, Ma,' I called towards the back kitchen.

Corporal Etheridge stood on the pavement, touched his cap and clicked his heels. 'The village has been secured, ma'am', he announced loudly for the benefit of all of us. 'I made sure I knocked on your door, Jean,' he added quietly.

Ma and Pa appeared from the kitchen, stepped into the street and surveyed the scene.

'It's all over, Mrs Muir,' said the corporal. 'We've posted guards here and there, as you can see.'

'Does this mean that we can hae oor village back?' asked Ma.

'We'll be gone within the hour, Mrs Muir. 'Back to camp.'

'Ony mair exercises in the village?' asked Pa.

'Strictly outside the village, sir, then we're back to camp at the end of the week.'

'And where's that?' asked Pa.

'Redcar,' replied the corporal, 'for more training, then who knows where.'

'All the best, corporal,' said Pa.

'Thank you, sir,' said Corporal Etheridge, smiling at me before he turned smartly on his heels and marched across the street to join a group of soldiers forming into ranks on the road outside the Ecclefechan Hotel.

I watched them march away towards the far end of the village.

I wonder how long I can use the address he gave me.

'Ye hardly know him, Jean,' said my Aunty Chrissie at teatime on the Friday after the mock attack.

'Aye, Ah ken. We've only promised tae write one another.'

'When'll ee see him again?'

'Nae idea, Aunty. Redcar is a hundred miles from Carlisle and a lot further from Birmingham. He should get some leave before he's sent overseas, so we'll see.'

'Aye, well dinnae rush intae onything. The war can dae funny things tae people.'

'He seems tae like me. That's the first man who's ever taken an interest.'

'Ee've never had much opportunity, Jean. Ah remember what it's like,' said my aunty. 'Ee dinnae hae much of a life when ee're in service. Ah never met onybody fi a' ma time in service.'

'Aye, Ah ken. Perhaps Ah should take a chance.'

'Whit, efter yin dance and a walk?'

'Several dances and two long walks. We talked and talked. Ah've telt ee, we've promised tae write one another, that's a'.'

'Yer accent's coming back,' said my aunty.

'Aye, the longer Ah'm in the Fechan, the more it comes back.

'Well, heed ma advice,' said my aunty while she cleared away the tea things noisily. 'Dinnae rush intae onything serious.'

'Ah wull,' I replied. 'Ah've always looked tae you. Ma and Pa have their hands full with the young uns. Ah'll nae bother them with ma goings on.' I picked up a dry tea towel from the rail above the range. 'Nae a word tae them, min.'

'Aye, yer secret's safe wi me,' said my aunty with a sigh. 'Yer auld enough tae know yer own mind.' She shot me a sideways look and with a shake of her head piled the remaining tea things into the bowl.

My first week's leave passed all too quickly. Whilst I felt the same sadness at leaving home as I did at Christmas, the prospect of returning to the drudgery of the factory was tempered by thoughts of Harry.

'Take a chance on him,' said Molly, on our way out of the canteen at dinner break on my first shift back. 'Us women might not get many chances while the war's on. If you like each other, that's a good start.'

'He might just want someone to write to while he's away from home,' I suggested.

'There's more to it than that, I reckon,' replied Molly. 'Right, let's get them lathes running.'

We pushed the rubber doors open and set to work. Harry's photograph in the top pocket of my overalls kept me going, gave me an extra purpose beyond doing my duty. Turning steel to make aircraft bolts for the foreseeable future took on a personal meaning greater than before. Harry and I were doing our duty together.

I wrote to Harry after I got up on Monday afternoon.

Will he think me too eager?

The lack of a reply suggested an answer to my constant fretting, until a letter arrived on Saturday morning during breakfast.

Mrs Ellsworth heard the letterbox rattle, put down her teacup and returned with a few envelopes, which she glanced at before leaving them on the sideboard apart from the one for me.

The writing wasn't my aunty's; I felt a twinge of excitement as I read the postmark: Redcar.

'I'll read it later,' I said.

*

The next time I saw Harry was in Carlisle on my way home for Christmas 1942, about four months after we got to know one another after the mock invasion of the Fechan. He managed to get leave for a day, catching a train to Newcastle for a change to Carlisle.

I met Harry off his train. I felt excited to be at the station, waiting for him to step onto the platform. Nothing like that had ever happened to me in my sheltered life. I felt a free, independent woman for the first time.

We embraced rather awkwardly on the platform while passengers gave us a wide berth respectful of the sight of a tender meeting between a soldier and his girl.

'I've only got an hour or so, Jean,' said Harry. 'Do you know a good place for lunch?'

'I used to work in Carlisle. The hotel opposite the station is good,' I suggested.

Our waitress was attentive and made a bit of a fuss of us, making me feel proud to be with my tall, smiley soldier.

'I'll be finished with training in a few months, Jean,' said Harry, looking at me over the rim of his teacup. 'Then we'll be posted. I don't know where. If it's overseas, I won't be allowed to tell you where. I hope that I can write though,' he added, placing his cup carefully on its saucer, a shadow of sadness wiping the usual broad smile from his features.

I felt his sadness, my throat tightening as he spoke.

'I've been thinking a lot since August,' he continued, 'thinking about you a lot, I mean.'

'Me too,' I replied. 'Thinking about you has helped me get through the long hours of the night shifts.'

Harry placed his hand over mine, glanced either side and leant forward as if he didn't want anyone else to hear. 'I know we've only known each other for a short while, so this is going to be rather sudden. But here goes. Will you marry me, Jean?'

Harry held me with his gaze.

My aunty's words came to mind, conflicting with Molly's.

'Don't answer straightaway. I know it's sudden, too sudden,' whispered Harry, leaning back in his chair.

The dining room seemed to take on a strange silence as if we were the only people in it cocooned in an invisible web.

What do I do?

'Can I think about it?' I said. 'Our lives have been turned upside down by the war. We're both away from home and—'

'Of course,' interjected Harry. 'We can wait until the war's over and then see.'

'I *will* think about it, talk to my older sister. She's not wed yet, so I'd be the first in our family to marry.'

'What about your parents?' asked Harry.

'I'll talk to them too, of course. Ma particularly. I'm the third of ten. Ma and Pa have got their hands full. They'll probably be glad to get us older ones out of the house.'

'Ten!' exclaimed Harry. 'Gosh.'

We walked back across the road to the station without speaking, my arm in Harry's. We had a lot to think about.

Another awkward embrace and a brief kiss left me standing on the platform, watching Harry's train draw slowly away, his disembodied hand waving furiously. I watched the carriages gather speed as they slid away from me before I crossed to my platform for the Lockerbie train.

I've grown up some more today.

Christmas weekend 1942 was a short leave from the factory. I returned to Birmingham on the Sunday, the day after Boxing Day in time for Monday's shift.

A letter from Harry at breakfast on the Tuesday let me know that he had a few days' leave at New Year, suggesting that we could meet in Birmingham while he changed trains for Cheltenham where his parents lived.

I replied immediately in the hope that he would receive my reply before he left Redcar on New Year's Eve in two days' time.

'I've got a couple of hours before my train home,' said Harry. 'I'm so glad you could meet me.'

'I've not got much time either,' I replied. 'My shift is at six thirty.'

The large station clock showed a few minutes before three.

'Of course, nights. What time do you sleep to during the day?'

'Oh, mid-afternoon as a rule. I got up early today.'

'Thank you, Jean. You won't be dropping off at work will you.'

'Not much chance of that. It's too noisy.'

We reached the top of New Street before Harry asked: 'Where are we going?'

'There's a Lyons just around the corner.' [22]

We were shown to a quiet corner table overlooking Victoria Square.

'A soldier and his girl,' whispered Harry. 'Always gets you a good table.'

We sipped tea and ate fruit cake, small talk masking what we both wanted to talk about.

'No, you first,' said Harry when we started speaking at the same time.

'I've been thinking about you,' I said, 'thinking about what you asked me.' I paused and took a deep breath. 'I accept your proposal.'

---

[22] Lyons (J. Lyons & Co.) first teashop (Corner House) opened in London in 1909 and developed into a chain of High Street teashops until the chain closed its doors in 1977.

Harry's trademark wide smile grew even wider. 'Then I've got something for you, Jean,' he said.

He drew a tiny box from his tunic pocket, opened it and held the box towards me. 'Like it?' he said. 'Let's see if it fits.' Harry pushed the ring onto my ring finger. 'Perfect,' he said, leaning back in his chair.

'It's lovely, Harry,' I said, adjusting the ring, turning it around my finger.

The delicate ring featured a diamond set in its centre with a smaller diamond at either side. My engagement ring was the first piece of precious jewellery I have been given, its significance and the occasion almost overwhelmed me.[23]

'Now we're engaged,' said Harry, beaming broadly.

'Congratulations,' whispered our waitress. 'I couldn't help noticing.'

'Thank you,' said Harry. 'Would you bring the bill, please.'

Harry leant forward. 'I didn't realise that she'd seen,' he said quietly. 'Sorry.'

'That's all right,' I replied. 'We can tell everyone now.'

'Let's see,' said Molly at the first tea break that night.

'It's in my locker, Moll,' I said. 'I thought it best not to wear it on the lathe.'

Molly and the girls crowded round me in the locker room at the end of the shift, taking it in turns to look at my outstretched hand.

---

[23] My mother wore the ring for the rest of her life. I have it in a box on the bookshelf in my study.

'Good on yer, Jean,' announced Molly, rounding off everyone's murmurs and nods of approval.

'Do you have a photo?' asked Lil. I showed her the one that Harry gave me. 'Ooh, handsome,' she said.

This pronouncement instigated another gathering of the girls, around Lil this time. More nods and murmurs of approval followed before Lil handed back the photograph.

'Well done, Jean,' said Molly. 'And it all started with a dance.'

'I'm not surprised,' added Madge.

'We'd better learn how to dance properly,' said Peggy. 'Might come in handy one day. Look what it did for Jean.'

Laughter and ribbing about menfolk occupied the final stages of washing and changing, marking the end-of-shift ritual for another night.

Chapter Twelve

"Make a good marriage"

Harry and I wrote to one another at least twice a week after we met on New Year's Eve. Our news was usually brief and often repetitive. His told in general terms about the rigour and tedium of training; mine was even less interesting: one night shift was very much like another. Despite our mutual lack of new things to tell one another, our letters always ended with tender thoughts and declarations of love.

Harry always expressed concern whenever I told him about the latest bombing raid.[24] His letter, following a raid in early 1943, announced that his regiment would finish training in early May and would be posted abroad. *Let's get married before I go,* he wrote.

I got engaged in the expectation that we would marry after the war ended. Getting married during the war would take some getting used to. Whether or not I was afraid that I might not see Harry again after he was posted, I agreed.

There was little I could do from Birmingham; no more leave was due until the summer. I wrote to Ma and Pa, and to Aunty Chrissie, asking them to make the necessary arrangements for Saturday 8th May, enclosing a large postal order. Harry wrote to his parents in Cheltenham.

---

[24] There were fewer raids in 1943 than at the height of the Birmingham blitz; they ceased altogether in April of that year.

All we could do was to leave the arrangements to others in the hope that everything would be ready for our wedding day.

The first few months of 1943 passed by quickly. I worked hard, earning good bonuses to save for our future as a married couple. Hope and dreams of a happy life with Harry spurred me on towards the day of our wedding. Excitement and anticipation of our wedding day conflicted with the uncertainty of the wait that would follow. After a day or two as a married woman, I would be parted from my husband for goodness knows how long. Our future happiness together would have to wait.

I tried not to dwell on the inevitability of being apart so soon after our wedding day. Our love for one another would hold us together, however far apart we were and for as long as it took for the war to end and bring Harry home to me.

Harry told me in one of his letters that he didn't think that he would get any leave once posted. *We'll be in the thick of it. Wait for me, Jean,* he wrote.

'A few of us are waiting, Jean. You'll be alright,' said Molly a few days before I left for home. 'Make a good marriage. Something good to look forward to when this lot's over.'

At the start of Monday's shift, Mr Collins called me into his office. 'So, you'll be leaving us, Jean.'

'Only for the weekend,' I replied.

'Ah, you didn't realise. Wives of servicemen are not required to undertake war work. At the end of this week, you will be a married woman. You will be free to go.'

'I didn't know that,' I replied.

'I understand why you asked for a day's leave on Friday. That's cutting things a bit fine. Where are we: Monday. Let's say that tomorrow is your last shift. You could travel home on Wednesday. More time to get ready for your big day. How does that sound?'

'That's very generous of you, Mr Collins. Thank you.'

'You have been a very diligent worker for the past two years. We will miss your contribution to what we do here for the war. You and Molly's gang are our best lathe operators. You'll not be easy to replace.'

'Thank you, Mr Collins. Molly taught me well.'

'She's a good one, our Molly,' said Mr Collins. He leant forward in his squeaky office chair and placed both hands on his desk. 'Come and see me after tea break on Wednesday morning and I'll settle your pay and savings.'

At dinner time on Tuesday's shift, Molly handed me a present, beautifully gift-wrapped. 'That's from all of us, Jean,' she said. 'A few things for your bottom drawer.'

Tears filled my eyes and the lump in my throat stopped me from speaking.

Molly and the girls were all looking at me, smiling and quietly wishing me good luck, all the best, and telling me that I'll be missed, sentiments that brought on more tears.

I dried my eyes and did my best to thank everyone around the dinner table, my voice strangled with emotion.

The hooter signalled the end of my final dinner break.

I worked more slowly than usual until the early morning tea break, my concentration drifting to thoughts of leaving friends made and departing Birmingham for good. Mrs Ellsworth had been very upset when I told her that I was leaving; she had no husband to wait for: I did. She was happier when I told her about my marriage, offering to accompany me to the city centre to buy a wedding dress.

'I can't afford to buy one,' I had told her. 'I'm going to borrow one. I won't need a going away outfit either. Harry has to be back on base on the Sunday.'

I thought about my landlady, alone and widowed. I thought about Molly and the girls, their laughter and high spirits.

Would I ever see any of them again?

All these thoughts tumbled around my head while I completed another batch of bolts until the hooter sounded.

'I have to go and see Mr Collins,' I told the girls a few minutes before the end of tea break. 'See you later,' I said, while standing at the end of our usual canteen table, holding my cup and saucer.

For a moment, Molly and the girls looked in my direction. Not a word was spoken; silence spread to other tables.

I looked around the canteen, feeling very self-conscious. Night after night, week after week for almost two years I had sat in the same place with a group of wonderful women. A wave of sadness swept over me, almost overwhelming me, tightening something in my stomach.

'Leave your cup, Jean,' said Molly. 'There's someone who wants to say something.

Maureen, the woman whose hair got caught in her lathe, approached from a nearby table. 'Good luck, Jean,' she said, hugging me tightly. 'You saved me.'

We held one another, unashamedly letting our emotions give vent to tears.

'Good luck, Jean,' came the chorus from around the canteen, followed by a ripple of applause as I made for the door.

I regained my composure by the time I knocked on the frosted glass-panelled door of Mr Collins's office.

'Sit down, Jean,' he said. 'Here's your Post Office savings book. You can take this to your nearest Post Office at home.'

I slipped the slim book that recorded my savings for the past two years into the pocket of my overalls.

'Your pay is made up for this week's shifts, plus a bonus based on this week's piece rate.'

'But I haven't finished tonight yet,' I pleaded.

Mr Collins held up a hand. 'Don't worry about that, I've taken that into account in the make up.'

'Thank you very much,' I said, pocketing the brown envelope.

'Please leave your work clothes in your locker with the key in the lock. Er, can I have your clock card badge back please. We are likely to need it.'

'How will I clock out?'

'No need to worry about that either. It's all been taken care of. You are free to go now. Are you okay getting to your digs at this time of the day?'

'I always walk, so I'll be okay. There's still two hours of work time to do though.'

'I've told you, you are free to go,' said Mr Collins with a smile. 'You have done your duty for your country. You can be proud of that for the rest of your life.'

Mr Collins stood, extended his right hand across his desk. 'Good luck, Miss Muir, and may I wish you all happiness in your forthcoming marriage.'

'Thank you, Mr Collins. You knew about that.'

'Of course, that's why you are no longer required to undertake war work: remember?'

'Oh, yes, of course,' I replied.

'This might be a large factory, but news can travel fast around here.'

Mr Collins held his office door open for me.

'Can I go down to the shop and say my goodbyes?' I asked him.

'Of course. Goodbye, Miss Muir.'

'Goodbye and thank you for everything,' I replied.

I pushed the rubber doors open and entered the shop, the racket of machinery crashed over me for the last time. I spotted Arthur working on an empty lathe. 'Goodbye, Arthur,' I mouthed.

'Goodbye, Jean,' he mouthed in return.

On my way back towards Molly's section, I said goodbye to Angus.

'A' the best, Jean,' he mouthed.

I stood on the opposite side of Lil's lathe, then Peggy's, Doris's, Madge's, mouthing my goodbyes to them all in turn.

Molly I left to last. She had seen me moving along the row of lathes and was wiping her hands on a rag when I stood on the opposite side of her motionless lathe. Molly cocked her head towards the doors of the shop. Once outside, we wept and hugged one another until our sobs subsided.

'Thank you for everything, Molly,' I said. 'You took me under your wing. I couldn't have done this without you.'

'Just you look after yourself and that husband of yours,' she replied. 'I hope you have a very happy life together when this wretched war is over. And come back and look us up when it is.'

'I will. I don't know where we'll live yet. I won't know until he comes home from the war. Molly, I hope that we'll see each other again one day.'

Molly gave me one more hug. 'Good luck, Jean,' she said quietly.

I watched her return to the shop, the opening of the double doors throwing out a blast of sound, only for it to be cut off as the doors settled back into position.

I stood alone in the outer entrance to the machine shop, the noise of the machinery a muffled whirr, then I turned and left the building and crossed the yard to the deserted locker room. After changing for the last time, I closed my locker, left its key in the lock and re-crossed the yard towards the main gate.

Shafts of dawn splintered across the sky above the city centre as I made my way to my digs, past the all too familiar bombed out factories and houses. By the look of it, it had been a quiet night; signs of new bomb damage were absent.

I felt fortunate that I would be leaving all this behind. The city that had been my home for two years faced uncertainty; Hitler's bombers were probably not finished with Birmingham yet.[25] My part in Birmingham's war was, on the other hand, at an end.

---

[25] Air raids over Birmingham came to an end in April 1943.

140

A chapter in my life had closed: another would begin on Saturday.

I had one more goodbye to make, to my wonderful landlady, Mrs Ellsworth.

Chapter Thirteen

Marriage in the Time of War

'Just a wee tuck here,' said Aunty Chrissie, through the side of her mouth, as she grasped pins between her lips. 'Keep still, Jean,' she mumbled.

Almost the first thing that happened when I arrived at the Fechan on Wednesday evening was the wedding dress fitting. Aunty Chrissie had suggested that I could get married in her wedding dress.

'Aye, ma Frank telt iss that Ah looked grand in it,' she said, extracting the final pin from her mouth. 'Such a shame he's no here tae see ee, Jean.'

I found no words to reply. Uncle Frank died suddenly at a young age.

'There, a' din. It'll no tak iss lang tae finish the final adjustments. Ye look grand, Jean.'

'Thank you, Aunty. Ah feel honoured to be wearing it.'

'Ach, away wi ee. Ah'll get on wi it while ee're away up the road.'

Ma busied herself with tea things while I told her about my last days at the factory. 'Pa still at his work?' I asked.

'Aye. He should be hame soon,' she replied.

No sooner Ma spoke, the front door opened. 'Yer hame, lass,' said Pa. 'It's good tae see ee. Ready for the big day?'

'As ready as Ah'll ever be. Thank you, both of you, for organising everything. Ah couldnae dae onything doon there.'

'Yer accent's comin' back again,' announced my brother William through a mouthful of tattie scone and jam.

'Dinnae speak wi yer mouth full,' I scolded.

'The Etheridge's arrive on Friday,' said Pa. 'They'll be stayin' ower the road. Ah've booked a room. We'll hae a wee get together ower there efter the church. Rationing's meant that lunch will be as best we can manage. A'body pitching in wi food and flowers.'

'How kind everyone is,' I said. 'Ah'm sure the day will go off fine.'

'And Harry is coming direct fri army camp,' said Ma.

'Aye, along wi his best man on Friday afternoon.'

'Ah've booked rooms fi them tae,' said Pa. 'And their best room fi the twa of ee fi Saturday.'

'Daes he hae tae garn back so soon?' asked Ma.

''Fraid so. He has to go back to camp on Sunday. They're being posted next week.'

'As soon as that,' said Ma. 'Yee'll only be wed for yin day.'

'Well, Ah'll just have tae wait for him tae come back,' I said.

I noticed a look pass between Ma and Pa. They held each other's gaze for a moment, leaving me wondering what lay behind it. I looked from one to the other. The moment passed, as if a shadow crossed the room between my parents.

'You'll be going over tae meet Harry's parents on Friday evening,' I said.

'Aye,' said Pa.

'Ah won't be able tae join ee. Harry'll be there.'

'Bad luck tae see each other the day afore ee wed,' said Ma.

143

'Ah'll stay at Chrissie's until Saturday morning. Ah'll be able to meet his parents then. How'm Ah getting tae Hoddom church?'

'John Johnson will tak the three o' iss in his taxi,' replied Pa.

'Taxi!'

'Fi nae charge,' added Pa.

'Mair kindness fri the folk of the Fechan,' I said.

'It's no every day we get a wedding wi a' the menfolk away at the war,' said Ma.

'Aye, right enough. Ah've captured ma soldier afore he goes off.' Again, the look between Ma and Pa flickered across the room. 'Ah'd better away, Chrissie's adjusting the dress.'

A chorus of 'see ee Saturday' echoed behind the closed door of my parents' terrace. I felt relieved to be spending a quiet day or two with my aunty away from the attention.

'Ah kin see ee're nervous, Jean,' said my aunty.

'It's a'wis a houseful up there,' I said. 'Ah'm glad of the peace and quiet here.'

My aunty stood away from me, admiring her handy work. 'A' din. Ee'll dae very nicely. Whit d'ye think?'

'It looks lovely, Aunty,' I said, looking down at myself.

'Ah havenae got a lang mirror, so this wee yin will hae tae dae.'

'The head-dress is perfect. Very pretty,' I added.

'Made it masell, Jean.'

'Ah cannae thank ee enough, Aunty.'

'Ach, away wi ee. Have ee eaten the day?'

'No much.'

'Well, Ah've a wee bit mutton stew left. Let's hae tea and a dram.'

*

With my older brother away at sea and my sisters Kathy and Danny unable to get leave, my younger brothers and younger sister joined Marion, and Ma and Pa to represent the Muir family at Hoddom Church. Everyone looked grand in their Sunday best as Pa escorted me slowly along the aisle to the church organist playing Here Comes the Bride.

Pa stepped back to make way for Harry. We glanced nervously at one another as we stood before the minister. Harry looked very handsome in his army uniform.

The emotion we felt could be heard in our responses, our voices cracking in reply to the minister's questions. Minister Calvin leant forward at one point, smiled and whispered: 'Nabdie minds if ye're baith nervous,' before he continued to conduct the service. We both felt a little calmer for the remainder of the proceedings.

Relief came when we signed our marriage certificate away from the gaze of the congregation. 'Well done,' said Minister Calvin. 'Ye can relax now.'

Harry smiled his broadest smile as he handed back the minister's fountain pen. 'Thank you for looking after us, sir,' he said.

'Just a moment,' said the minister. He signalled to the organist. 'Swap sides, that's it. Ee are ready tae go. Take it slowly.'

My husband and I walked slowly along the aisle to the joyful sound of the Wedding March. Everyone was smiling in our direction. My face began to ache with the effort to maintain a smile in return. Ma and Pa Muir and Ma and Pa Etheridge looked full of joy as we passed the front row of pews.

He looks like his dad.

We gathered outside the church door for a photograph, with Harry and his family, and his best man, to my right, and the Muir family to my left.[26] The photographer insisted that we carried on smiling during what seemed like a very long exposure. 'Thank you, everyone,' he said at last. 'All done.'

The group began to break up, happy chatter dissolving the ache in my face.

Harry introduced me to his parents.

'You look lovely, Jean,' said Ma Etheridge.

'Indeed you do,' added Pa Etheridge.

'Thank you,' I replied.

More introductions and lively exchanges followed for several minutes until Pa and Robert, Harry's best man, began to urge everyone to make their way to the Ecclefechan Hotel. 'You and Harry go with John Johnson,' said Pa.

'Congratulations t'ye baith,' said John, turning to face us from the driver's seat of his taxi. 'We'll wait fi a few minutes until a'body's gaen, then we'll garn the lang road roon tae the hotel. We cannae hae Mr and Mrs Etheridge arriving first.'

Harry held my hand as we sat in the back of John's taxi. 'Gosh, I didn't expect to be that nervous,' he said.

'We both were,' I replied. 'I could hear it in your voice.'

'We got through it okay though. The minister was very kind. He helped us calm our nerves.'

'It went well,' I replied. 'This is a happy day for me.'

---

[26] This is the photograph referred to in the Prologue (on page 4).

'Me too,' said Harry. 'Me too,' he repeated, giving my hand a firm squeeze.

'I'm looking forward to getting to know your mother and father,' I said.

'They you too,' Harry replied. 'It seems strange that you've only just met.'

'Well, that's the war,' I suggested. 'It's kept us apart until today.'

'And will do again tomorrow,' said Harry, a gloomy expression accompanying his flat tone of voice.

'Let's not think about that just yet,' I said. 'Let's enjoy today.'

'A'reet, let's away,' announced John suddenly.

Harry leant towards me. 'I don't quite catch everything people are saying,' he whispered. 'I've never heard anything like the local accent.'

'I'm used to it, of course,' I said. 'Mine comes back when I'm here, well partly. You're doing fine.'

The back room of the Ecclefechan Hotel looked splendid. Vases of flowers were dotted here and there, balloons hung over the door, and a home-made banner attached to the foot of the refreshment table welcomed Mr and Mrs Etheridge.

I wonder who made that?

A ripple of applause greeted us as John held one of the double doors open. 'Thank you for taking us there and back, John,' I said.

'Ma pleasure, Jean,' he replied.

'Wull ee hae some refreshment?'

'Ah cannae stop, Ah've got a fare in Annan.'

'A'reet.'

'Good luck tae ye baith now.'

We stepped into the room as man and wife, happy to mingle with each other's families. Most of the menfolk already had pints of beer in their hands. The womenfolk waited patiently while hearty sips were taken, glasses were found spaces on tables and orders for drinks for the womenfolk were taken, almost emptying the room of the men.

All eyes were on Harry and Robert when they returned from the front bar carrying trays of drinks. Harry handed me a schooner of sherry. He looked tall and handsome in his uniform, smiled expansively at anyone who approached him and seemed happy to enjoy being the centre of attention.

'He's a handsome fella', whispered Aunty Chrissie.

'Aye, he is so,' I replied.

'Just ee hang on tae that yin,' she added.

'I'll try,' I said. 'We'll not be together until the end of the war though.'

'Aye, Ah ken. Absence wull make it stronger,' said my aunty. 'Yee'll see.'

By late evening, Ma and Pa Etheridge, Ma and Pa Muir, Harry and I were the only ones remaining in the wedding breakfast room nursing our night caps.

'Harry and I want to thank all of you for arranging everything in our absence,' I announced, raising a half-empty schooner.

'Me too,' said Harry, sounding rather tipsy as he raised his empty beer glass.

'It was all done by David and Kate,' said Ma Etheridge. 'We couldn't do much from where we are.'

'Well, it's been a grand day,' I said.

We chatted for another hour or so. Ma and Pa Etheridge asked me about my war work: they seemed genuinely interested in what I learnt to do for the war effort.

'We're very proud of the both of you,' said Pa Etheridge.

'My wife has done her bit,' said Harry. 'Mine begins next week.'

Quietness settled over our table while we dwelt on what my husband reminded us about.

'Good luck, son,' said my Pa. 'Tak guid care o' yersel.'

'I will do, sir,' replied Harry. 'I'll be back to take care of your daughter.'

Harry looked at me. 'Wait for me, Jean. I'll be back when it's over.'

Tears misted my eyes. Harry handed me a handkerchief. 'Sorry, love. I didn't mean to—'

'It's okay,' I said. 'I'm okay.'

'I think we'll turn in now,' announced Harry. 'I've a train to catch in the morning.'

We said our goodnights, leaving our parents to continue chatting.

I followed Harry upstairs to our room, feeling more nervous than I had in church. I knew what would be expected of me, but I had little idea what it would be like. I was completely inexperienced in such matters.

Ma had put out a nightdress from my suitcase that I brought up from Birmingham; my case stood on the floor at the foot of the double bed. Harry unbuttoned his army tunic with one hand and rummaged about in his suitcase with the other. Neither of us spoke; we could feel each other's uncertainty.

'Jean,' said Harry as he draped his tunic over the back of one of the chairs. 'I know that this is supposed to be a special night for us. How do you feel though? Be honest.'

'Nervous. I'm inexperienced. Well, no experience at all actually.'

'Me neither,' said Harry, with a sigh of relief. 'To be honest, I've had a bit too much to drink to be of any use to you in any case.'

What can he mean?

'Let's save ourselves for when I get back to you and there's more time to get to know each other properly, for this I mean. Do you mind?'

'Of course not,' I replied. 'I'm rather relieved, to be quite honest.'

'Well, that's us being honest with each other That's got to be a good sign, hasn't it?'

We tried to fall asleep in each other's arms, content to be intimate in a small way. Nevertheless, it took me longer to drop off than Harry. Sharing a bed with another person was something that I hadn't experienced since us bairns shared a bed at Ma and Pa's terrace. Lying in the arms of a sleeping man was so utterly strange, so undeniably expected, sanctified by what we said in church a few hours earlier. Despite the formality and legality of our marriage vows, it didn't feel natural to be sharing a bed so soon after we had hardly begun to know each other.

Harry continued sleeping soundly when I disentangled his arms from around me. It made it easier for me to go to sleep when he turned over, barely breaking the rhythm of his deep breathing. I could feel the warmth of him, the latent strength of him as I snuggled into his back. There would be ample time for lovemaking when he came home to me after the war. I would simply have to be strong and hold on to the promises we made to one another: Harry married me; he chose me.

I would wait for him, wait to experience loving him with my body as well as my heart. We chose to start our married life this way. Whatever the war threw at us, we would survive. Our marriage would lie in wait, ready to begin anew and last into the future.

Now, at this moment, in this darkened hotel bedroom, my indeterminate period of waiting began.

'Goodnight, Harry,' I whispered. 'Come back soon, my dear. Don't forget me when you go to war.'

The next morning was punctuated with saying farewell to the Etheridge family. John Johnson was ready with his taxi directly after breakfast to take Harry, his best man and Harry's parents to Carlisle for their trains.

'Write to us, Jean,' said Ma Etheridge.

'And come and visit,' added Pa Etheridge.

'Goodbye, Jean,' said Robert, hugging me politely and giving me a brief kiss on the cheek.

'There's room free in the front,' John said to Harry.

'Well, that's me off then,' said Harry, taking me in his arms. His army tunic felt rough against my wet cheek. We held one another for a long time, Harry's embrace smothering my shaking body.

'Wait for me, Jean,' he whispered. 'And think of me.'

'I'll be thinking about you all the time, longing for the end of the war,' I replied, disentangling myself and looking up into his blue-grey eyes.

Harry cupped my still damp cheeks with his hands, wiped away a falling tear with his lips and turned away from me. He turned back just as he opened the front door of the taxi, gave me one of his broadest smiles and pulled the door shut.

John Johnson set off noisily along the High Street towards the Carlisle Road. I watched and waved until I could no longer see or hear the taxi.

My husband had gone to war. I didn't know when or if I would see him again. I had to hang on to hope, hope that would help the passage of time, hope that Harry would survive the fighting, hope that we could begin our future as husband and wife before too long.

Sunday morning in the Fechan fell silent. Ma and Pa stood a discreet distance away from where I parted from Harry; Chrissie stood outside her terrace across the road.

The machine shop suddenly felt a very long way away; the war returned to its distant reality. I was home, my duty to the war effort complete. I had no idea what I would do with myself until the war came to an end. Anxiety and uncertainty troubled me. How long would I have to wait; how long before we could be together, be in love, have children?

I didn't know the answer to any of these questions; they unsettled me and would not let go of me.

Chapter Fourteen

My Years of Waiting

Waiting for the end of the war became an ache that I tried to hide from my family. Only Aunty Chrissie knew how I felt. Living with her, rather than at my crowded parents' house, meant that it was almost impossible to conceal the sadness within me; the sense of loss of my husband crept through the mask of attempted cheerfulness from time to time.

'It feels as if Ah'm a widow, Aunty,' I would say when I felt at my worst.

'It'll no be fi ever, Jean. Buck up now. Yer making me sad an a'.' Her usual reply shook me out of my melancholy, helping me to remember that my aunty *was* a widow.

I didn't want to go back to domestic work. I saved my allocated portion of Harry's army pay; we would need it and what I had saved from my war work. Instead, I took orders for dressmaking and knitting. Wool was easy to get hold of at the large haberdashery in Carlisle and second-hand dress material was readily available. I visited the market in Lockerbie regularly and haggled with stall holders, usually coming away with frocks that I could reuse, as well the occasional part-bolt of unwanted material.

Making clothes to order took my mind off my ever-present feeling of anxiety. I worked hard, spending long days in my aunty's back parlour on her ancient Singer sewing machine.

Pa gave the machine an overhaul at the start of my venture; thereafter, it only needed his occasional attention. My reputation grew until, after about a year, I was forced to turn work away for the next twelve months.

Altering wedding dresses for the daughters of their first wearers made me particularly sad. Nevertheless, I took special care with them and helped my aunty with fitting when the young bride and her mother came to our terrace.

'Another soldier's wedding,' said my aunty after another successful fitting. 'Just like you, they'll be waiting,' she added, as if talking to herself as she tidied up her boxes of pins.

News of the war was sparse in our local newspaper. Very few families in the Fechan owned a wireless and hardly anyone took a national (Scottish) title. Despite the lack of hard facts, we gradually gained the impression that the war in Europe was turning in our favour.

I received a letter from Harry every few months or so. He couldn't tell me anything about the progress of the war directly. Instead, I tried to read between the lines to ascertain what he referred to as "a bad day" really meant. He usually told me how he was feeling, what he thought about army food: *The same thing every day,* and always took the trouble to ask about my family before he signed off: *All my love, Harry. Thinking about you.*

I always wrote back immediately. Sometimes, his next letter acknowledged mine, sometimes not. I merely assumed that if he was on the move letter deliveries might be unreliable.

Just before Easter of 1945, a letter arrived from Harry: no return address had been added at the top. The letter was brief, telling me that I might not hear from him for a while. He ended with:

We're on the move again. Things are happening here.

I hope to see you soon,
  All my love,
  Harry.

Thinking about you always. I can't wait to hold you in my arms.

'Fri Harry?' asked my aunty.

'Aye. He says that Ah might no hear fri him for quite a while,' I replied.

'Wonder whit that means,' said my aunty quietly.

'Then what *The Standard* says is true,' I suggested.[27]

'Ah jolly well hope so,' said my aunty. 'Let's hope that our menfolk are back hame soon.'

About a month after receiving Harry's letter, I was in Carlisle delivering a cardigan to an elderly lady. I caught sight of a news-stand near the bus stop for the bus home:

GERMANY SURRENDERS

---

[27] *The Dumfries and Galloway Standard and Advertiser*, a local paper at the time.

exalted the poster.

I queued for an early copy of the *Cumberland Evening News*, read and re-read the front page whilst on the bus to Ecclefechan.

Excitement at the thought of seeing Harry soon became tinged with sorrow. The loss of husbands of my fellow workers at the factory, and the grief of my landlady flooded across my feelings for Harry. I had been lucky, or I assumed that I had been: no news from Harry must mean that he had survived the war.

News of Germany's surrender had spread to our sleepy village by the time my bus drew into Ecclefechan. Pa read the front page of the newspaper to Ma and the bairns.

'They'll a' be hame soon,' said Ma.

'And Harry?' asked Pa. 'D'ye ken when he'll be hame?'

'Nae idea,' I replied. 'All Ah can dae is wait tae hear something fri him.'

Word spread that the Prime Minister would speak to the nation on Tuesday afternoon at three o'clock.

'The hotel's got hold o' a wireless,' said Pa. 'We'll garn ower and listen.'

The moment that Winston Churchill announced that Germany had surrendered, the hotel bar erupted with cheers that no amount of shushing from Michael, the landlord, could subdue.

Bunting, Union Jacks, and the Scottish Saltire had already appeared up and down the High Street. The elderly menfolk spilled out of the hotel, holding their pint glasses aloft, singing and cheering wildly.

I followed Ma and Pa out of the hotel. We pushed our way through the throng of men, women and children, and escaped to our front parlour.

'Jean, away tae fetch Chrissie,' said Pa. 'We'll a' hae a dram.'

'Here's tae the future, a better future,' said Pa, raising his glass when I returned with her.

'We'll a' drink tae that,' added my aunty.

Glasses were clinked, refilled and clinked again. Pa's best whisky gave us a warm glow inside, sufficient to quash my anxiety about the immediate future: when and where would it begin?

I was twenty-seven years of age when the war ended. Would married life with Harry be the only thing I could look forward to? I had spent many years in domestic work. I worried that being my own housekeeper was my only prospect in life, along with motherhood; there was always motherhood to look forward to. I had seen my mother change shape enough times. I was the third of ten: I knew that I had no intention of spending year after year bearing children, but becoming a good mother and a loving wife would have my full attention.

'One fi the road, Jeanie?' said Pa, jolting me out of my thoughts.

He's been a guid faither tae us a'.

'Aye, even if the road is short,' I replied.

Pa leant forward and poured a large measure of honey-coloured liquid into my empty glass.

'No post free again the day,' said Ma when I looked in on her later in the week. 'It'll tak time fi the men tae be sent hame,' she added. 'Dinnae worry.'

I did worry, despite my parents' reassurances. I couldn't understand why I hadn't heard anything.

It wasn't until July that news of men returning to our village spread quickly. 'The Davidson brothers are back,' said Aunty Chrissie. 'And Mrs Murray's boy.'

'That's guid news,' I replied. 'Shows that something's happening.'

'Ye'll hear something soon, Jean. Dinnae fret.'

I was working on a dress repair when my aunty came into the back parlour. She put a mug of tea next to the sewing machine and handed me a letter. 'Yer Ma just brought this f'ree,' she said.

I took my foot off the treadle and held the letter. My hands shook as I read the postmark: Cheltenham. Ma and Pa's address wasn't in Harry's writing though.

What can this mean?

'Ah'll leave ee tae it,' said my aunty.

I opened the envelope slowly.

Perhaps it's bad news.

I read the content quickly, then slowly.

The letter was from Ma Etheridge. Harry had been demobbed from his unit and will be arriving at Birmingham New Street Station on Friday 13th July at two fifty for a connection to Cheltenham. He hopes that you will meet him in Birmingham.

Why didn't he write to me?

I dashed into the kitchen. 'He's hame, Aunty, he's hame!'

Aunty Chrissie crushed me in a huge hug. 'Ah, that's such guid news, Jean. At last.'

'His train gets intae Birmingham on Friday afternoon. Ah can't wait to see him.' I sat at the kitchen table, clutching my letter.

'Ye'll be leaving iss again, then,' said my aunty.

'Ah suppose we'll live with Harry's parents until we can get somewhere of our own. Goodness knows how lang that will be.'

'There's hardly ony work aroon here,' said my aunty. 'Ah suppose he's got mair chance of getting a job doon there.'

'He drove buses afore the war. He'll probably try and get his old job back.'

'Ee'll be away the moran's moran then?'

'Aye. Ah'll catch a train fi Carlisle on Friday morning.'

'The bairns'll be at the schuil when ee garn?'

'No. Ah'm away early, but Ah'll go aroon teatime tomorrow and say ma goodbyes.'

After school the next afternoon I went round to see Ma and Pa. 'Yee'll see me off in the morning,' I said. 'Ah've booked John Johnson.'

'What about us?' chorused my younger brothers and sister.

'Ah'm away before schuil, so ee can see iss off,' I replied.

'Wull ee let the others know where Ah've gone?' I said to Pa.

'Aye. We're expecting 'em ony day,' replied Pa.

'Tell them a' Ah'm sorry Ah missed 'em,' I said. 'Ah'll write when Ah'm settled. See ee a' in the moran,' I called out as I opened the door onto the street.

John Johnson's taxi drew up outside Ma and Pa's terrace on the dot of seven o'clock. I could see him cleaning the windscreen as I took the few steps along the High Street from my aunty's terrace.

'Ah'll say goodbye here, Jean,' she had said. 'Ah dinnae think Ah kin dae it wi a' the others.'

'Ah can't thank ee enough, Aunty. Ee've been so good tae me.'

Another embrace brought on tears for both of us.

'Ach, away wi ee,' my aunty said. 'They'll be waiting.'

Ma hugged me tightly, barely able to speak.

Pa's embrace was brief, his face a cloud of sadness. 'Look efter yersel, Jeanie,' he said. 'Yer hame is elsewhere the noo.'

Pa's parting words tied the knots in my stomach tighter. Four years ago, I had said goodbye to my home and family to face the unknown. Now it was happening all over again, this time facing a future as a married woman, equally uncertain.

Looking from face to face, I suddenly felt the urge to be on my way, scarcely able to burden my emotions with any more farewells. Marion, my younger brothers, and sister Betty managed silent waves as Pa closed the rear door of the taxi.

'A'reet, John, I said.

Pa turned, a faint smile softened his features as he looked at me through the glass. He wasn't to know that I could lip read. 'Ah'll a'ways be yer faither,' he whispered.

I turned to look back along the High Street as the taxi drew slowly away. The Muir family gathered in the middle of the road, waving and calling out their messages drowned out by the noise of John's taxi.

I watched them until we reached the Carlisle Road where a bend closed my family from view. I turned to face forwards, imagining them standing for a moment, wondering what to do next. Soon, Ma and Pa would return to the routine of their day and the youngsters would go to school. I didn't know what my routine would be, what I would do in the days to come. The thrill of seeing Harry replaced the overwhelming sorrow of leaving home again.

'A'reet, Jean,' said John.

'Aye. Ah'm fine, John,' I replied.

Anticipation grew the closer we got to Carlisle. When I left home to work in Birmingham, I imagined that it would be a temporary parting; when I left home this morning, it would be for good. My new home would be somewhere else; my life would be with someone else. I had gained parents-in-law I didn't know. I would have new responsibilities to them and to my husband.

I would face whatever life threw at me in the aftermath of war, determined to make Harry happy, have children and carve out a future for ourselves. My family would always be there, in the Fechan, in the background. Today's train journey would be the first stage of me stepping forward to my new life.

John set me down outside the railway station and put my case on the pavement.

'A' the best, Jean,' he said.

'Thank you, John,' I said as I paid the fare.

I watched him drive away, then picked up my case: my new life beckoned.

Chapter Fifteen

Scenes From a Married Life

It felt very strange to be waiting inside New Street Station instead of catching a bus to Smethwick. As I sat on a wooden bench, my thoughts turned back two years to Molly and the girls, to my landlady and to my brief life as a factory worker. Here I was once more in the city that kept me away from home; this time I had arrived as a married woman, anxious and excited.

I found out the platform number where Harry's train was scheduled to arrive at two fifty. Every few minutes, my eyes were drawn to the large clock suspended over Platform 2. Time seemed to slow down as the minutes ebbed slowly away.

Just after ten minutes past the hour, a cloud of smoke and steam announced the arrival of a noisy engine.

Is this it?

I stood and watched the coaches drift by as they slowed down gradually. Doors flung open and spilled dozens of passengers onto the platform. Excitement gripped my stomach; my throat tightened.

Where is he?

I suddenly realised that I was looking for Harry in his army uniform.

Keep looking.

Then I saw him, waving vigorously several yards along the platform. We battled through the crowd of hurrying passengers until we were face to face. Harry dropped his huge kitbag and clasped me in his arms.

We held one another in a silent embrace, while people stepped around us. My heart thudded, vibrating in my throat, my breath came in gasps accompanied by tears.

Harry held me by my shoulders. 'It's good to see you, Jean,' he said, smiling broadly. 'Three years is a long time.'

'It's good to see you too,' I spluttered through my sobs. 'I didn't recognise you at first. I was looking for you in your uniform.'

'All over now, Jean. They gave me this suit,' said Harry, tugging at the lapels. 'It'll do for now.'

He's a lot thinner.

'Have we time for a cuppa before our train?'

'Yes, let's do that,' I replied.

Harry slung his kitbag over his right shoulder, picked up my case and we went in search of refreshment.

Harry's parents had prepared their spare room for us with pretty furnishings and a double bed. 'It's our wedding present to you both,' said Clara. 'You are welcome to stay here until you find a place of your own.'

'Thanks, Mum,' said Harry. 'Though I wonder how long that will take us straight after the war.'

'Settle in and come down for tea when you're ready. Dad'll be home soon.'

'This is a lovely room,' I said. 'Your parents are very kind.'

'It'll do until we get somewhere,' said Harry dismissively. ''We can't stay here indefinitely.'

Further conversation ended abruptly as we unpacked our clothes and hung them in the large wardrobe.

'Neither of us has much,' I observed, breaking the silence.

'Yeah, not much to get started with,' rejoined Harry. 'Everything we have is in this room.'

'I've got one or two things for my bottom drawer,' I said.

'Better put them in there, then,' said Harry sharply, showing no interest. 'Jean, I need to get my old job back. I'll go to the depot in the morning. Cash is what we need.'

'I'll get a job as well,' I said.

'I'd rather you didn't work,' said Harry, glaring at me.

'Why ever not?' I replied. 'I've worked all my life. I don't propose to stop now just because I'm married.'

'That's just the point,' said Harry, flinging his empty kit bag on to the top of the wardrobe. He turned to face me. 'Married women don't work. They keep house.'

'We haven't got one to keep.'

'You can help Mum.'

'Of course I will. That won't keep me occupied for long. We both need to earn a wage.'

'Let's drop it for now,' said Harry wearily. 'I've made my view clear. Let's go down.'

'You think you'll be able to just walk in and ask for your old job back,' said William, facing his son across the dining table.

'They'll be laying off the women drivers. Stands to reason,' replied Harry.

'Bit of a shame for the women,' added Clara. 'They'll lose their wage.'

'Lose it to the menfolk coming back,' insisted Harry. 'Besides, they can go back to being conductresses.'

'Bus conductresses already are mostly women,' said Clara.

'And some old blokes,' said Harry. 'They can go, make room for the women drivers to transfer and make room for us. Simple.'

'Well, we'll see,' said William. 'Good luck for tomorrow.'

'What about you, Jean?' asked William. 'You've kept out of this so far.'

'My last job was dressmaking, alterations and the like,' I replied. 'There might be something in town where I could get work.'

'Come into town with me in the morning, Jean,' suggested Clara. 'I'll show you the ladieswear stores. You could try there.'

Harry said nothing as he shot me a disapproving look across the table. We had spent barely one afternoon and evening at Harry's parents' house and we had argued.

I don't care what he thinks. I'll show him I can earn too.

Harry was correct: women bus drivers were being laid off. He got his old job back, starting with late shifts the following Monday on his previous route. I got work at Miss Shills Drapery Shop in Bath Road, not dressmaking but using my sewing and machinist skills

165

making and adjusting curtains four and a half days a week including Saturday mornings. Working part-time gave me the opportunity to help Clara cook and keep house.

'Take no notice of Harry, Jean,' said Clara after I finished my first week at the shop. 'He's living in the past. He's no idea how women kept the country going for the past few years. Well, some idea, but he thinks that he can turn the clock back.'

'There's the door. That'll be Pa,' I said.

'Harry must be eating at the canteen at the garage of an evening,' said Clara. I detected the disappointment in her voice and in the way that she looked at me.

We certainly don't see much of each other.

'Ready to dish up?' said Clara, carrying plates through to the dining room.

I was asleep when Harry got home after his late shift later that evening. He snapped the bedroom light on, waking me with a start.

'Sorry to wake you,' he whispered, pulling back the bedclothes on his side of the bed.

I turned to face the wall, shielding my eyes from the ceiling light. I heard Harry putting his clothes away before he switched off the light and slid into bed. A cold hand grasped mine; I felt his breath against my neck.

'Not now, Harry. You stink of beer.'

'When then?' he whispered.

'When your parents are out of the house and you don't breathe beery fumes all over me.'

He must go to the pub at the end of every shift.

Harry sighed, turned over and muttered something. I couldn't make out the words; perhaps I wasn't meant to. Neither was I in the mood to find out.

I had shunned Harry's advances earlier that week when an almost identical scene played out. I feared that this would happen again, a feeling that troubled me sufficiently to keep me awake, listening to Harry's deep breathing.

I fell asleep eventually, despite an image of Harry laughing, drinking and smoking in a noisy pub with his mates from the bus depot. I imagined myself looking in at the door without entering, willing Harry to look towards me. The persistent image turned into a dream. I had conjured it up in the first place, but my mind must have taken it over while I slept. The next thing I remembered was Harry looking up from his pint glass, glancing towards the door, then turning away to talk to someone at his table.

I woke the next morning feeling troubled by the dream. I sat up in bed; Harry slept soundly despite my waking.

He ignored me. Did I imagine it or did I dream it?

I went down to breakfast, leaving Harry in bed. We rarely saw one another at breakfast apart from on Sundays. I usually left the house for work while Harry got up late. By the time I returned, Harry was well into his late shift, returning home after we had all gone to bed.

Our respective working arrangements meant that Saturday afternoons and Sundays were the only time we saw one another for any length of time. Most Sundays, Clara helped at a nearby Sunday school and William played bowls, leaving the house and us alone, properly alone. As autumn drew in, William's bowling season came to an end, further limiting opportunities when Harry and I could pretend to be husband and wife in our own home.

'I hardly see you,' I said, one Sunday afternoon in October while we lay in bed. 'William won't be out on Sundays soon, so we'll be together even less,' I complained. 'Can't you change your shift?'

'Better money, Jean. We need a place of our own. When're you going to the council next?'

'I pop out from work every Monday lunchtime,' I replied. 'There's nothing yet. We're on a list, but I bet it's a long one.'

'What about private?'

'Clara and I scour the ads every week. There's nothing that we can afford.'

'Well, I wonder how much longer I can carry on here,' said Harry.

'What do you mean?' I said, sitting up, hugging my knees.

'Mum and Dad are very kind, of course they are, but it's not the start I wanted,' said Harry. 'I'm going to get up. They'll be back soon.'

'Me neither. What did you expect straight after the war?'

'I don't know; I don't know,' grumbled Harry as he gathered up his clothes. 'I'm just off for a quick wash.'

I waited until I heard Harry go downstairs before getting dressed. I looked at myself in the bathroom mirror. An unhappy face looked back at me, reflecting how I felt most of the time. Grabbing hurried moments of intimacy, always listening for the sound of the front door wasn't my idea of a married life. Equally, I didn't know what to expect in the aftermath of the war. At least we had a home and at least we could be a married couple from time to time.

That night the scene that I thought I'd imagined, plagued my sleep. It really was a dream this time, ending in the same way: Harry looks up from his drink, makes eye contact with me and then looks away. I step backwards and close the door of the noisy pub. The vivid dream recurred several times during the months that followed. Sometimes I woke, my heart thudding, accompanied by a feeling of anxiety; on other occasions I remembered the dream later in the day.

'Are you feeling all right, Jean?' asked Clara at breakfast on the first Monday in December.

'I didn't sleep that well,' I replied.

'Me neither. It's getting chilly at night. We can't afford to heat upstairs.'

'It's all right, Clara,' I said, attempting to sound cheerful, thrusting the dream into the back of my mind. 'Harry is like a giant hot water bottle.'

'More than I can say about William. His feet are always freezing *and* he hogs the water bottle.'

'I'll go out and buy two more at lunchtime today,' I said.

'I thought you always called at the Housing Office on a Monday,' said Clara.

'I'll do both,' I replied. 'I must be off. See you at teatime.'

'Any luck at Housing?' asked Clara over a cup of tea when I returned later that afternoon.

I shook my head.

'Don't worry, dear. Something will turn up.'

*

Something didn't look like turning up for the rest of December, a situation that only served to increase the tension between Harry and me and played upon my state of anxiety, a state of mind that I tried to hide whenever Harry and I had the house to ourselves.

'You seem to be having trouble relaxing,' said Harry one Sunday afternoon near Christmas. He was getting dressed and spoke to me while facing away from me.

'I'm sorry,' I replied. 'It's our housing situation—'

'Or lack of it,' said Harry, as he bent down to tie his shoelaces.

'It's playing on my mind.'

'I can tell there's something bothering you. It bothers me too. I'll see you downstairs. Let's get the tea things out before they get back.'

The other thing that bothered me, as if I didn't have troubles enough, was that Harry made it clear that he was dead against me going to the Fechan for Christmas. 'Your place is here, with me,' Harry told me every time I raised the subject.

I could see Harry's parents' embarrassment whenever the subject of Christmas came up during a weekend meal, usually the only occasion when the four of us sat down together at the dining table. Harry's fervent reaction was always the same.

I resigned myself to the realisation that I wouldn't be home at the Fechan for Christmas. Whenever I thought about it, I felt homesick just as I had felt during the war. I decided that I would visit home in the New Year, whatever Harry commanded.

As it would turn out, no such visit took place in the New Year.

*

170

Christmas at the Etheridge household was a rather stilted affair. I occupied myself in the kitchen helping Clara prepare meals. Her sister, Mavis, spent Christmas Day with us, so at least the presence of another member of the family broke the atmosphere of unspoken conflict.

We had little to give to one another, agreeing that exchanging presents amongst the four of us would not be the sensible thing to do, our austerity reflecting that felt more widely in the country. Instead we pooled our resources and provided the best Christmas dinner that we could manage.

Clara and I put up home-made trimmings and decorated a Christmas tree that William and Harry brought home. I tried to be cheerful, but deep inside I felt unhappy. I did my best not to show my sadness, hoping that my mask of forced jollity hid my real feelings sufficiently. From time to time over the Christmas period, I suspected that Clara knew that I was showing a brave face: occasional glances in my direction were full of understanding and sympathy.

The morning after Boxing Day came as a relief. Harry had a reduced shift that day and I had two days before I went to work in the shop on the last Saturday of the year. I decided to wait until Christmas and New Year festivities were behind us.

January came and went before I thought about broaching the subject. In the event, I waited until the worst of the winter weather passed. It was well after Easter when I mentioned my planned trip to Harry; his reaction remined unchanged.

I pleaded with him to explain why he was so adamant. 'I haven't seen my family for months. You could come with me.'

Harry left the breakfast table without a word. I heard the front door close.

'I'm sorry, Jean,' said Clara. 'I don't know what's got into him.' I helped her clear away the breakfast things. 'He doesn't start until this afternoon,' said Clara with a sigh. 'Where's he off to at this time on a Saturday?'

'All I want to do is see my family for a few days,' I said.

'I know, dear,' said Clara. 'Any news from Housing?' she asked, changing the subject.

'We might be in a better position if we had children,' I replied. 'That much is clear from what they tell me about the list.'

Clara glanced at me; her hands deep in the sink ceased their rapid wiping motions. I stood, poised with a tea towel, waiting for the next item to dry. 'Nothing in that department yet, Ma,' I said, feeling my face tingle with redness. 'We're trying though.'

'It must be difficult for you, living with us I mean. You probably don't get many opportunities,' said Clara, returning her attention to the next plate to wash.

'We manage,' I replied quietly. 'I feel that it will happen eventually.'

Clara turned to face me again, smiled and patted my arm with a soapy hand. No further words were exchanged on the matter during the remainder of the washing up.

Tomorrow would be Sunday, two weeks since my last period was due in late May. I could have told Clara after breakfast. However, I decided to wait until the following day; I could tell Harry first then tell William and Clara later.

Harry came home late on Saturday night as usual. I could tell immediately that he had been to the pub after work. I left him while he had a lie in at breakfast time.

Harry got up just in time for Sunday lunch, so I had no opportunity to give him the news first. It would have to be announced to the whole family.

'An excellent lunch, Clara,' said William, patting his tummy.

'Jean is a great help, as usual,' replied Clara.

'Thank you, Jean, added William. 'What would we do without you.'

'You might have to soon,' I replied.

'What do you mean?' asked William.

'Well, Harry will soon be a father and you will be grandparents.'

The room went very quiet as the news sunk in.

'I couldn't tell you yesterday, Ma. That wouldn't have been fair to Harry. I was asleep when he got in last night, so there was no opportunity,' I said, looking across at my husband. 'Anyway, you all know now.' Harry appeared to be unmoved by my announcement.

'This could get us up the housing list,' I suggested, looking around the table.

'Wonderful news, Jean,' said William.

'Yes, it is,' rejoined Clara. 'Congratulations to the both of you.'

'Thanks, Mum,' said Harry, avoiding eye contact with me. 'There won't be room for a child, so I hope that we can get somewhere soon.'

'Why didn't you tell me first,' complained Harry when we were getting ready for bed that evening.

'I only knew for certain a day or two ago. You're out so much, I couldn't find a chance to tell you. What difference does it make? I thought that a family announcement might be nice.'

'It made a difference to me,' said Harry as he turned away from me on his side of the bed, signalling an end to the conversation.

I lay awake, staring at the ceiling in the darkness. I worried about the way that Harry had reacted; I could not tell if he was happy to find out that he would soon be a father. Doubts plagued my mind until my head ached. Not for the first time did the notion that I had made a mistake dawn upon me, a terrible mistake with my life. I silently cried myself to sleep that night.

At breakfast the next morning, Harry announced that he had a few days holiday owed. 'I'm going to Hastings to visit Gran,' he said.

'Take Jean,' suggested Clara.

'I don't think I could get leave at such short notice,' I said.

I could see that Harry was relieved. 'Besides, she best not travel in her condition,' he said.

Towards the end of that week in June, I found Clara opening a letter at the breakfast table. 'It's from Harry. What's he doing writing. He hardly ever writes. I hardly ever heard from him from Redcar. Did you, Jean?' Clara turned the pages of the letter. 'Not bad news about Mum, I hope,' she said.

I didn't reply to Clara's question while she read the letter.

'Oh, he's found somewhere to live,' said Clara suddenly, her voice lifting at the news.

That's more than I've managed.

Clara dropped her arms to the table, rattling her plate and knife, jolting me out of my thoughts. Her left-hand shook, still holding the letter tightly. Clara stared at me, her eyes wide, her mouth open and rigid as if her lips were paralysed.

I put my half-drunk cup of tea carefully on its saucer. 'Whatever's the matter, Ma? Is it your mother?'

Clara shook her head slowly from side to side. I thought that would never stop.

'No,' she said, almost in a whisper. 'No, it's not that.'

'What then?' I asked.

'He's found somewhere to live all right, but not with you, Jean. Not with you and the baby.'

A burning sensation overwhelmed my throat, my chest tightened and instant tears blurred my vision.

Clara's voice shook. 'My son, my son, what have you done.' She dropped the letter onto the table, pushed her chair back and came round to where I sat shaking and sobbing. I put my arms around her waist and buried my head in her chest. Clara held my head close to her, while the shock of Harry's letter took hold of me. We remained in this awkward position until my weeping calmed enough for me to speak.

'I don't understand,' I spluttered. 'Where did I fail to live up to his expectations? I've given him a child. I thought that was what he wanted. Now he doesn't want to stay with me even for the sake of our child. Where did I go wrong? Where—'

'Shh now, dear,' said Clara. 'Try not to take on so. I'm going to the phone box to phone William. You'll be all right for a few minutes?'

I nodded.

Clara picked up the letter and left the room. I sat rigid with shock, unable to grasp the suddenness of Harry's revelation. Barely a week had gone by since I told everyone that I was pregnant; now I'm told second-hand that Harry is leaving me. My growing fear that I might have made a mistake had turned into a stark reality. I had indeed made a grave mistake, one that I would have to live with for the rest of my days. These things turned over and over in my head while I waited for Clara to return.

'He's on his way,' she announced, putting her head around the door.

'How can he leave work?' I asked.

'They've said that he can come home,' replied Clara. 'Don't worry. He'll be here soon.'

Clara busied herself while I stayed sitting at the table, as if paralysed. I didn't know what to do with myself, with my baby, with my mind. My life had been brought to an abrupt stop, at the behest of two sheets of blue writing paper and had fallen into a chasm, into a void where I felt only numbness.

I felt helpless, utterly helpless and bereft, plunged into a sadness that I had never felt before. I felt sorry for myself, for my unborn baby, for my in-laws. As for Harry, I didn't know how I felt apart from numb and angry. We had barely been together as a married couple for a year; now he had deserted me and our child. And all this in the face of his cowardly behaviour. He wrote to his mother, not to me. His cruelty towards me struck a deep wound in my heart.

I must have remained at the table for a very long time. Clara cleared the breakfast things away, working around me. 'Don't get up, Jean. William will be … at last.'

My father-in-law entered the room. 'Show me the letter,' he said to Clara, after glancing in my direction with a shake of his head. 'Cheltenham postmark: that's a lie. He said he was going to Hastings. This explains his recent behaviour.'

William crossed the room, still holding the envelope and letter, pulled up a chair and sat next to me. He laid a hand on my wrist. 'Jean,' he began. 'I hardly know what to say. Our son has lied to all of us and has acted cowardly and despicably towards you.' Colour drained from his cheeks as he struggled to maintain eye contact.

'Does he say anything about me?' I asked.

William glanced at the letter.

'The other page,' said Clara.

'Is that it: "Sorry. Tell my wife that I'm sorry."' He read. 'He's about to become a father and that's all he has to say.'

William left the table and began to pace the room from side to side. 'Pretty obvious where he's been all week,' he muttered.

'Who is she?' I asked quietly.

'Someone at work, at the depot, I'd guess,' replied William. 'Explains all the late nights. Oh, this is just awful, absolutely awful … unforgivable. We're at a loss, Jean.

'I don't want to be here when he gets back,' I said.

'I can't imagine him coming back here now,' said William. 'This all seems pretty final.'

'He'll be wanting his things, though,' said Clara.

'He won't be coming back here today if I've got anything to do with it. I'm going to the garage right now.'

'It's too early for his shift, isn't it?' said Clara.

'I'll wait for him if I have to,' replied William.

'Do be careful,' pleaded Clara.

'I just want to talk to him,' said William. 'Give him a piece of my mind.'

William looked across at me as he held the door open. His lips moved as if to say something. Instead he shook his head again, handed the letter back to Clara and left the room.

'I don't want to be here when he collects his things,' I said.

'Oh, Jean, what a terrible situation,' said Clara. She sat opposite me, clutching Harry's letter. 'What will you do?'

'I will go home to Scotland and have my baby,' I replied.

'You don't think that you're being too hasty?'

'What else can I do? I can't stay here. Even the thought of it is painful.'

'All right, dear. You know best. Whatever happens we will always love you. You won't forget us will you?'

'Of course not. You've both been so very kind to me. You'll see your grandchild one day. I'll see to that.'

I didn't see William until breakfast the following day. At first, he sat stony-faced, without speaking.

'Did you see him?' I asked.

William nodded. 'I had to go back later and wait until the end of his late shift. He came out of the depot with a bunch of blokes and a woman, a conductress probably. When he saw me, he said something to the others and crossed the street. We just stared at one another for ages. "I'm not coming home, Dad," he said. "You've left Jean pregnant," I reminded him. "We can't talk here," he said. Then he re-crossed the road to join his mates and left me standing there, fuming to myself. I'll have to have a talk with him another time.'

'You won't be able to change his mind,' said Clara.

'Probably not. But he's not getting away with this without a piece of my mind ringing in his ear. He's got to turn up here at some time or other.'

'Jean is leaving too,' said Clara.

William looked at me; his face still held a shadow of anger from recounting the brief meeting with his son.

'I'm going home to have my baby,' I said.

'You won't have it here in Cheltenham?'

'No. This place is dead to me now. I'm very fond of the both of you, but I can't stay here.'

'I understand,' said William. 'What about our grandchild?'

'I'll bring him to see you when he's old enough to travel.'

'Him?'

'Oh, did I say "him"? Or her, then.'

'When will you be leaving?' asked William.

'Tomorrow.'

'So soon,' said William, glancing at Clara.

'Would you find out the trains, please. I'll need a connection in Birmingham to Carlisle or Lockerbie.'

'I'll look that up for you today.'

William leant back in his chair, folded his napkin and placed both hands on the table. 'Of course, we wish that you would stay with us, but we respect your wish to return home to Scotland. I'll get off to the station now. See you both at teatime.'

I spent the remainder of the day in our bedroom, occupying my mind by sorting through my belongings.

I stood on a chair and took my suitcase down from the top of the wardrobe, laid it on the unmade bed and flung the top open. 'I didn't think that I'd be needing you like this,' I said aloud.

I placed the few summer clothes that I possessed in the case: a rather faded frock, two blouses, and two black skirts. My undergarments and spare nightdress went on top as well as the tablecloth, still in its tissue paper, given to me when I left the factory. Ample room remained for toiletries and my makeup bag to be packed in the morning. Personal bits and pieces would go into my large shoulder bag-cum-handbag. I would wear my summer coat for the journey home.

I decided to leave my old green overcoat behind, along with all my winter woollies: there wasn't enough room for them in my case.

I wanted to travel light; I would have to lug my case around all day, so sacrificing some of the clothes that I had bought in Cheltenham would be necessary. Leaving my winter clothes behind was an easy loss to bear: I just wanted to go home, get away from this town, this room, this unhappy period of my life.

I closed the case, put it on the floor and lay down on the bed; my mind raced with questions: no answers came, no explanation as to where I had gone wrong, where I had made Harry turn away from me.

At length, I felt a strange sense of relief and calm. My short marriage was at an end; there would be no going back. I placed both hands on my tummy. 'It's just the two of us now,' I whispered to my growing child. 'You'll have no father; just me.'

I must have slept until mid-afternoon. Clara told me later that she had put her head round the bedroom door to see if I wanted any lunch. 'I left you to it, Jean,' she said when I came down.

'I've left my winter clothes in the wardrobe, Ma.'

'Oh, do you want them sent on?'

'No, it's okay. My old coat is pretty faded. Can you make use of them at the next church jumble sale?'

'If you're sure, dear.'

'There's something else that I'd like you to do, if that's okay.'

'Yes, dear.'

'Would you explain things to Shills please. Not all the details, but would you say that I'll be leaving and won't be coming back. I'll write and explain why I didn't work my notice properly.'

'I'll do that, of course, Jean.'

'I'm a week in hand, so would you ask them to send my money on, or you could. I've got a Post Office account, so a money order sent to my mother's address should tidy things up.'

'I'll tell them tomorrow. Leave it to me.'

William was very quiet at tea later that afternoon. He didn't say much until the end of the meal. 'I've ordered a taxi for the morning, Jean. I've written down your train times and platforms. Your train north stops at Ecclefechan.' William handed me a slip of paper.

'Thank you, Pa,' I said. 'Saves me a bus from Carlisle or Lockerbie.'

After Clara and I cleared away the tea things, Clara picked up her knitting and I read the local newspaper.

'He's gone to the depot again,' said Clara after we heard the front door close. 'He's taken this very badly, Jean. We both have.'

'There's little I can say, Ma. I've got to resign myself and accept that it's over. I can't get over the suddenness, but I know that Harry wasn't content. All those absences. I thought that he cared for me, but I was wrong. I made a mistake, now I'm paying for it.'

My mother-in-law laid her knitting in her lap, pulled a handkerchief from her sleeve and dried her eyes. 'This would have been for the baby,' she said, choking back more tears.

'It still can be, Ma. It still can be. Please finish it and send it to me when it's ready. A warm, woolly blanket will be very welcome for my bairn.'

William pressed a pound note into my hand after he put my case into the back of the taxi. 'You sure you don't want me to come to the station,' he said.

'I'll be fine,' I replied. 'I'd best say my goodbyes here.'

'That's to pay for the taxi fare,' said William. 'Goodbye, Jean,' he added, hugging me briefly.

William stood aside to let Clara clasp me tightly. 'Write soon, Jean,' she said, her voice shaking with emotion.

'I will, and thank you for everything, for putting up with me this past year. I'll miss you both.'

I got into the taxi quickly, to delay further would make it even more difficult to say goodbye. William closed the rear door, spoke to the driver and waved briefly; his faint smile faded rapidly as the taxi drew away from the Etheridge's house.

I turned around and waved at the retreating figures waving back until the taxi turned a corner, shutting my in-laws out of sight.

Now I really am on my own.

Waiting for my train in Birmingham felt very strange. I recalled my first visit during the war when I felt anxious and rather scared of leaving home to begin my war work. I thought about the last time I waited here. Instead of feeling frightened, I had felt excited at meeting Harry back from the war. How very different these two occasions were. And now, here I was again, on the move once more, saddled with deep sadness, tinged with resentment and a supressed anger that I reserved for Harry, a resentment that I felt towards the way my life had turned out now that he had abandoned me and our unborn child. Harry was the source of my failing hope, my bitterness towards the world.

I sat on a wooden bench on Platform 2, oblivious to the noise and smell of the busy station, unaware of who came and left the bench. I willed the minutes to pass so that I could go home.

It was dusk when the train drew into Ecclefechan station. I waited until the light of the guard's van disappeared, leaving me standing on the empty platform. I could hear the train's engine become fainter as it steamed the few miles to Lockerbie until all was quiet where I stood, my case beside me. It had been a long day, a long journey. In a short while I would be home and there would be some explaining to do.

I wondered if Ma or Pa Muir had ever arrived alone at this station in days gone by, and what circumstances had drawn them home.

I picked up my case, ascended the steps to the main road and set off for the village. I had no choice but be truthful to my family: my husband had abandoned me while I fell pregnant.

I reached the Thomas Carlyle monument at the top of the hill that descends into the High Street and paused for a moment. The sight of the darkening village lifted my sagging spirits. Yellow light leaked from windows not yet curtained, as if to welcome my unexpected homecoming.

'Home at last, my wee one,' I said aloud. 'Let's away and tell them what's happened.'

I started the descent of the hill, in the hope that I would reach my aunty's terrace before anyone saw me. A soft light filtered through the curtains of her front parlour. I knocked on the front door in the hope that she would answer quickly. I wanted to avoid explaining my arrival with a suitcase to anyone passing. A glance up and down the street confirmed that there was nobody about.

Aunty Chrissie opened her front door. 'Jean,' she said. 'Whit're ee dain—'

'Can I come in?' I said quickly. 'I can't face Ma and Pa the night.'

'Whatever's the matter? Come away in.'

I left my case and shoulder bag just inside the front door and almost fell into one of the armchairs near the hearth.

'Ee look worn oot, Jean. Have ee eaten?'

'No for hours.'

'Right. Ye just stay there.'

My aunty went into her back kitchen, emerging after a few minutes with a tray. 'A cup of tea and a scone,' she announced. 'Noo, tell iss whit's garn on.'

I told my aunty the ins and outs of my time in Cheltenham between mouthfuls of delicious freshly baked tatty scone and sips of strong tea. I tried to explain how my doubts about Harry began shortly after we moved in with his parents.

'I don't know where I went wrong,' I said, my voice catching in my throat. 'I've made a terrible mistake, Aunty. Terrible. I'll have to live with it.'

Aunty Chrissie pulled a handkerchief from the sleeve of her jumper and handed it to me.

'Thank you,' I said, wiping at my tears.

'So he just up and left ee with his Ma and Pa?'

'They were furious with him. I came home as soon as I could. I didn't want to see him again after the way he's treated me.'

'Seems like ee did the right thing, coming hame tae the Fechan.'

'That's not the end of it, Aunty. I'm pregnant.'

My aunty Chrissie shook her head and winced silently. 'Oh, Jean, that's cruel of him,' she said. 'So cruel.'

'I feel betrayed. He didn't want to stay for the sake of our child.'

'Wid ee want him tae?'

'No. He left me for another woman. I'm obviously not good enough for him, a disappointment I suppose.'

'Ee mustnae think that, Jean. Ee'll mak a guid mother.'

'Aye, well, if I do, then I'll do it on my own.'

'Dearie me, Jean … dearie me. Now, listen. Have ee had enough tae eat?'

'Yes, thank you, Aunty.'

'Get yersel away tae yer bed. Yer room is still made up. Ee can see yer Ma and Pa in the moran.'

'Aye, I will. I can't the night.'

'Whit'll ee tell 'em?'

'Whit Ah've telt ee,' I said, turning halfway up the stairs.

'Yer accent's coming back,' said my aunty. 'Jean,' she said as I reached the tiny landing. 'This is the place. Ee'll be a'reet here.'

'Aye,' I replied. 'Night, Aunty.

Chapter Sixteen

My Early Post-War Years

My Post Office account enabled me to give my aunty a weekly contribution to my upkeep. I didn't earn any money during the autumn of 1946; instead, I relied on my not inconsiderable savings to keep me going. I had hardly touched what I earned and saved during the time I worked in the shop in Cheltenham for almost a year, topped up by what they owed me when I left suddenly in the summer.

I helped Ma with my younger siblings and did what I could to help at my aunty's, both women nagging me to take it easy as my tummy grew during the autumn months.

I planned to find work somehow where I could take my child after I gave birth in January.

'Ah'll look efter the bairn, Jean,' said Ma a few days before Christmas.

'Ah cannae ask ee tae dae that, Ma.'

'Ah've din so wi ten. Another yin'll nae mak ony difference. Besides, there's just the three bairns at hame noo.'

'Ah ken, but it's time ee had a break fri child rearing. Don't think Ah'm no grateful. Let's see whit happens in the New Year. Ah'll get work. Ah'll have tae. Talking of which, that's their tea ready. They'll be hame fri the schuil presently.'

Ma finished cutting bread.

'Is everyone coming hame fi Christmas?' I asked.

'Ah dinnae ken fi sure. Some dinnae write often. Let's prepare for a house full.'

I set to work preparing a stew for Ma, Pa, and me for later.

Domesticity had tempered my feeling of bitterness and disappointment to some extent since I fled Cheltenham. I knew it wouldn't last. I would be a mother soon. Another mouth to feed would be a heavy responsibly upon me. I would need to earn for two. I fretted constantly how I could do so with a child to look after. I had long since stopped imagining that my husband would provide for us. It would be up to me: somehow, I would face up to the challenge ahead.

My sisters would go on to make successful marriages: I hadn't; something that set me apart. I had to prove to them and to my Ma and Pa that I could be a good parent without anyone else's help.

Not for the first time did these things pursue my thoughts as I busied myself with the evening meal.

*

'Aye, Jean, ee'll no be lang noo,' said Ma a few days before Hogmanay. 'Just a few days mair,' she added.

I sat near the fire, watching Ma make tatty scones, just as I had done when I was a child. I felt tired and awkward; reaching full term made me feel guilty: there was little I could do to help Ma.

'It's snowing again,' I said.

'This is an awfy winter, Jean,' said Ma, looking up while she kneaded dough.

'How'll Ah get tae Dumfries?' I said.

'Dinnae worry. We'll get ee there,' Ma replied.

I wasn't convinced. The sight of large flakes of snow almost obscuring the view onto the Hight Street only heightened my anxiety.

'At least Pa has got work clearing sna,' said Ma.

'Ah can hear shovels just now,' I said.

'It's a constant battle keeping the streets clear,' said Ma. 'Ah hope the coalman can get here the day.'

It had snowed constantly since mid-December. The men of the village kept the Hight Street and other roads clear daily; the Lockerbie Road was kept clear by the Council for the benefit of farm vehicles and milk collection. Pa kept us informed as to what was clear and what was blocked when he finished for the day.

Apart from clearing snow, there was very little work for the men, a situation made worse by post-war austerity. Ordinarily Pa sought work on local farms. Since the start of the long snowfall, farm work had all but dried up. Cattle and sheep were dying from the cold and winter crops froze in the ground. Pa was often called upon to help load dead cattle onto wagons, work that he didn't like to talk about.

Somehow we muddled through the first weeks of the winter of 1946. We were careful with our meagre coal supply and food was far less plentiful than in the summer. Pa had stored potatoes and greens harvested from the small plot behind the terrace. I had helped Aunty Chrissie with her plot until she barred me from bending to work in her garden. Despite our best efforts to store vegetables for the winter, our food supply began to deplete.

Hardship and hunger returned to the Muir household during that dreadful winter. My memory flew back to the time when my sister and I begged for coal from passing trains. I stared out of the window, wondering why we hadn't come very far or progressed since the days of poverty that characterised my childhood in the 1920s.

The thud of dough on the kitchen table brought me out of my melancholic thoughts.

'Yer miles away, Jean,' said Ma as she shaped a tatty scone.

'Aye, so Ah was,' I replied. 'And there'll soon be another mouth tae feed.'

'Dinnae worry yersel,' Ma said, wiping floury hands down the front of her apron. 'We'll get by.'

Although I slept at my Aunty's house, I divided my time between her and Ma's house, helping with meals as best I could. Tinned goods were available from the corner shop, where the owner, Mr Hosborough, introduced a rationing system, explaining that he didn't want to run out between irregular and erratic deliveries. Flour was subject to stringent rationing. Mixing it with potato was a tried and tested way to make a bag of flour last longer if it was used to make tatty scones. We didn't make a loaf of bread for months.

A let up in the fall of snow in early January meant that the roads in and around the village could be cleared completely, leaving huge banks of snow several feet high along either side of the High Street and adjoining roads.

'Whit's the main road like, Pa,' said my mother after she had cleared the table after a simple lunch on the first Tuesday of the month.

'Huge drifts, but clear in places,' replied Pa. 'Are ee a'reet, Jean?'

Tuesday 7th of January 1947 remains firmly fixed in my memory. I felt instinctively that I was close.

My mother came over to where I was sitting by the newly made-up fire. She felt my forehead, my tummy, and my pulse. 'Contractions in the neet?' she said.

I nodded. 'Ah think we need to garn,' I replied.

'Pa, go and fetch John Johnson.'

Pa dashed out of the door, returning a few minutes later.

'He's on his way,' he said, gasping for breath. 'Ah'll no tak ma bits off. Ah'll away oot front and wait fi him. Get Jean's things, Ma.'

Ma and Pa helped me into the back seat of the taxi.

'Stay here, Davey,' said my mother. 'There'll be the boys tae see tae.'

'A'reet, ladies,' called out John. 'Let's away.'

John took the shorter of the slopes out of the village. 'We'll garn bi Lockerbie, Kate,' he announced. 'The road'll be clearer than cutting across through Dalton tae the Dumfries Road.'

'Aye, we're in yer hands, John,' said my mother.

We huddled together as John turned right onto the Lockerbie Road. Drifts of snow several feet high towered over us on both sides, leaving a gap just wide enough for two vehicles where the road had been cleared.

The Lockerbie to Dumfries Road was worse. Long stretches of snow lay on the road, despite the high drifts on either side. The taxi slewed from side to side as John tried to follow the tracks of unseen vehicles.

'Dinnae fret, Jean. Ah'll get ee there,' John called out, barely audible over the noise of the taxi revving up as if in protest.

Yard by yard, mile by mile, John struggled up and down the hilly Dumfries Road.

'Looks like Lochmaben is clear,' he announced as we drove through the village only to meet what looked like a blocked road. 'Only a few miles mair,' he called out to us. 'Are ee a'reet, Jean?'

'Aye,' I replied.

John battled through the shallowest parts of the snow until the road became clearer.

Thank goodness.

'That's better. Must be mair fairms here,' called John.

'Aye, there are,' replied Ma.

'Ah dinnae ken why that bit back there wis si bad,' called John. 'Oh, it's snaing again.'

The windscreen wipers flicked to and fro in what seemed a losing battle. John leant forward, peering at what was left of the road ahead almost invisible from where we sat in the back seat, huddled together as tightly as we could, too frightened to say anything.

Those last few miles to Dumfries agonised and stretched; I closed my eyes, shutting out the weather and let the loud drone of John's taxi give me hope.

As long as we keep going.

'Hooses,' cried John.

I opened my eyes. The outskirts of the town came as a huge relief. A hazardous journey of twenty miles had taken us almost three hours. At last, John had clear streets into Dumfries town.

'Here's the Cresswell,' said John, drawing to a stop opposite the entrance away from the parked ambulances.[28] 'Ah'll away in and tell 'em whit tae expect.'

John helped me out of the taxi, grabbed my bag and ran into the maternity hospital. We followed slowly, my mother supporting me with an arm around my back.

We met John as we stepped through the entrance doors. 'Ower there,' he said, pointing. 'They've got yer bag.'

'Ah cannae thank ee enough, John,' said my mother. 'Ah'll settle up wi ee when Ah get hame.'

'Ach, dinnae worry about that the noo, Mrs Muir. Ah'm just awfy glad Ah got ee here.'

'Be careful garn back,' I said. 'And thank you, John. Ah'll never forget what ee did.'

'Ach, away wi ee. Ah'll away hame. A' the best, Jean.'

I turned to watch John step into the fading afternoon light as another contraction wracked my body, sending my hands flying to my distended stomach. My cry of pain brought a nurse to my side.

'Come along, dear,' she said with a smile. 'You're in guid hands now.'

We were only just in time. My son was born about an hour after we arrived at the Cresswell, at five minutes past five on Tuesday 7th January 1947. I named him David Muir, after my father.

My son was probably the warmest soul in Ecclefechan during the remainder of the horrendous winter of 1946–1947. Snowfall began again in earnest a week after he was born and continued until late March. The

---

[28] The Cresswell Maternity Hospital closed in 1948.

snow drifts that John Johnson drove miraculously through to get me to hospital grew even higher as the roads were cleared with the help of the army.

I looked forward to the day when I could tell my son that he was born during one of Scotland's severest winters after I was driven to hospital in conditions that almost defy description.[29]

Aunty Chrissie kept a fire going by day and kept it low at night. I slept downstairs for a few months near to my son who slept in a wooden cot made by Pa. It mattered little who was in the room; David's cot remained close to the fire until the weak March sun revealed the land under snow that had lain for months.

David would have no memory of the harsh winter of his birth. My recollection of that awful winter is with me to this day.

*

'Wull ee no stop pulling the chain,' cried my mother from the foot of the stairs. My three younger brothers, my only siblings still living with Ma and Pa just over a year since my son was born, clattered up and down the stairs, dashed in and out of the fitted bathroom and could be heard arguing about who would be sleeping where.

A small estate of new houses occupied land just above the village to the east of the High Street. The Muir family were among the first families to move in,

---

[29] She did tell me, often.

taking Number 2 Ashgrove Crescent, the first plot on the right at the top of the hill.[30]

The favourable end position meant that Ma and Pa had a large triangular patch of land on one side of the house. It wasn't long before Pa planted several rows of potatoes, carrots, onions, and greens. There were still several mouths to feed, including David and me, along with older siblings who stayed from time to time, home from far away work.

'Ee'll a'wis hae a room here, Jean,' said Aunty Chrissie on the morning of the move.

'Don't ee want tae leave this old terrace, Aunty?' I asked.

'Where ee are garn is fi families. Ah'm alane, so Ah'll stay here.'

'Well, Ah can't thank ee enough for putting iss up fi a' this time. There's room for David and me in the new house. Ah think Ma and Pa wull like having their grandson at home.'

'And you.'

'Ah suppose so,' I replied. 'Just between you and me, Ah'm going tae have tae get work somewhere soon, and a place of oor ain. Somewhere fi ma son tae grow up.'

'Aye, he is bonny, Jean,' said my aunty, gently touching David's nose. 'Remember what Ah said: there's a'wis room for the baith of ee here if it gets crowded up there.' David smiled up at my aunty and burbled contentedly. 'Are ee a'reet carrying him a' that way?'

---

[30] The house and the original estate remain to this day, the latter much expanded.

'It's no far. The cart has gone up for the last time. Ah'll away and see whit's garn on.'

'See ee later then,' said my aunty. 'Ah'll come and hae a nose round the new hoose.'

I could see that Ma and Pa were very excited with their brand-new council house. In the space of a morning, they left behind an old terrace with rudimentary means of washing, cooking, and keeping warm and took possession of a new house with its proper bathroom and kitchen.

'Nae mair water pump,' cried Ma as she turned the tap on and off over the kitchen sink.

'And nae mair cooking ower an open fire,' added Pa.

'Look,' said Ma. 'The electric oven even has a hot plate tae dae scones.'

'This is grand,' I said.

'We're very fortunate,' said Pa. 'Only a few families are in the new hooses. The builders are still ower the road. I'll make mair furniture, Ma,' he added. 'We'll get by wi whit we've brought up fi noo.'

Pa and the boys busied themselves unpacking boxes and moving chairs around, once Ma had stemmed my brothers' excitement relishing their first experience of a flushing lavatory.

'Ah want ee doon here, you three,' cried Ma from the kitchen. 'Away oot and help Pa sort out the rest of oor things. And use the front door,' she yelled as my three younger brothers dashed past her and out of the side door of the kitchen. 'That'll keep 'em busy while we hae a rest,' said my mother as she flopped into one of our only two armchairs. I put David down as soon as his cot was brought into the large living room.

'It's a wonder he's slept through a' this,' said my mother.

'Aye, he's a good sleeper. It'll be time for his feed soon.'

A brief silence descended on the room. We could hear Pa and his pal who owns the cart carrying beds upstairs.

'Something good's come oot o' the war,' said my mother. 'Decent hooses for the likes of us for yin thing.' She looked around the room, slowly taking everything in as if in a dream. 'Ah'm still pinching masell. A proper oven an a'. Hot water from a back boiler. A real bath!'

'Aye, it's grand, Ma. Ah'm proud of ee baith. You deserve a proper place tae live.'

'And there's room fi ee and the bairn.'

'Aunty has been very generous this past year or two. But it's nice to be really hame.'

'Breaktime ower,' announced my mother, heaving herself out of her chair. 'David's greetin and the men'll be wantin' mair tea.'

Chapter Seventeen

Dora Walker: a Woman of Consequence

'Ee'll stay at Danny's,' said my mother as she watched me pack my well-travelled suitcase again.

'Aye, Ah wull. Just room for some of David's things this time. Ah'll send some money if Ah get the job, so ee can send on the rest o' ma claes.'

'Ah'll miss ee, Jean. A'body's leaving hame.'

'Ah'll miss ee too, and Pa. It's tae get work, Ma. There's little work hereabouts.'

'Aye, Ah ken … Ah ken. At least some of oor young yins are close by.'

'Onyway, it's an interview. Ah might be back yet.'

'Come doon when ee're ready,' said Ma. 'Ah'll keep an eye on David.'

I had answered an advertisement in *The Lady* magazine for a live-in housekeeper at an address in Birmingham. I had plenty of experience of domestic work prior to the war to draw upon, enough for me to feel qualified as a housekeeper for someone else; it was what my education and pre-war years seemed to have decided and determined how I would earn a wage. At that period of my life, a few years after the end of the war, no other option seemed to be open to me. After all, I was a single mother with a child to look after. I worried that my potential employer would reject me out of hand; she might not want to have someone with a small boy in tow.

Ma and Pa bade me goodbye as if I would be leaving for good.

'It's an interview, Pa,' I persisted. 'Ah might be back in a day or two.'

'Give oor love tae Danny and Tommy,' said Pa, hugging me tightly. 'Look efter yersel and the wee un.'

How many times had I left the Fechan, facing an uncertain future: I had lost count. This time, I had a three and half year old sitting by my side, waving with me as the Carlisle bus drew away from the bus stop in the High Street, leaving Ma, Pa, and Aunty Chrissie standing on the pavement, watching and waving until the bus turned up Academy Street where we lost sight of one another.

This time it might be for good.

My sister Danny met us at New Street station in Birmingham. 'You're showing a lot now, Danny,' I said while we waited for a bus.

'Aye, I'll have to stop work soon,' she said. 'Tommy has a good wage at the Austin. We'll manage.' [31]

My sister and her husband lived in a prefab near the Queen Elizabeth hospital; I would be able to walk to Mrs Walker's house in Hintelsham Avenue for the interview.[32]

'Are ee taking David?' asked Danny when I got myself ready the following morning.

'Aye, the only way to find out if she'll have the both of us,' I replied.

---

[31] The site of the Austin Motor Company, based in Longbridge in Birmingham, was redeveloped as a business park in 2005.
[32] Prefabs (prefabricated homes) were constructed to address the post-Second World War housing shortage.

David was understandably feeling tired after the walk to Hintelsham Avenue. A mile must have felt a long way for a little boy to walk.

I wiped his face and brushed his hair with my hands before we crunched our way up the short drive to Number 18 and knocked on the front door.

The noise of the large, heavy door knocker echoed deep within. I stepped away from the door and held my son's hand.

I should have put gloves on him.

'Why are we here, Mummy?'

'We've come to visit …'

A young woman opened the door. 'Mrs Etheridge?'

'Yes.'

'Please come in. This way,' she said, leading the way along a wide hallway to a room on the right.

The woman knocked, opened a door and spoke to someone. 'They're here, Gran.'

David and I waited in the hall.

'You can go in now,' the woman said.

Her grandmother sat in a high-backed armchair. She seemed to be enveloped in lace and a large shawl; rather severe spectacles dominated a face lined with age.

'I hope that you don't mind if I've brought my son,' I said.

'Not at all. Please sit opposite me,' she replied. 'Your letter said that you have a child.'

The elderly lady's voice sounded cultured; someone who I would call "well-spoken". David stood next to my chair, almost hiding behind me.

'Hello, little man,' she said quietly.[33]

'Don't be shy, son,' I said.

David peeped out from behind the chair. 'Hello,' he whispered.

'Mrs Etheridge,' began the lady. 'Would you fetch down that box on the shelf behind you.'

'This one,' I said.

'Yes. Slide the lid off and put it on the carpet over by the window. Your son can play with the bricks if he likes.'

The large box contained a great many smooth, shiny beautifully made wooden bricks of various shapes and sizes. David was soon absorbed with making shapes, dismantling them and re-making them. The view through French windows of a large garden stretched away from where David sat on the carpet, busy with the box of bricks.

'Now we can have a chat,' said the lady. 'Doctor Robertson gave you a very good reference, by the way.'

'Oh, that's nice of him. I could only provide one reference for a housekeeping job. Then the war stopped all that.'

At that moment, the young woman who had let us in brought a tray of tea things.

'Would you leave it on the table please, Amanda.'

'All right, Gran,' she said. 'I'll leave you to it.'

'Would you like some tea?' the lady asked.

'Thank you,' I replied. 'How do you take your tea?'

'A little milk. No sugar.'

Is this a simple test?

---

[33] This is what Mrs Walker often called me, according to my mother.

I poured two cups of tea, placed the lady's on the small round table at her right elbow. I held my cup and saucer in my lap, stealing sips between answers to the lady's questions.

Very elegant china.

Mrs Walker asked me about my duties at the doctor's house before the war, about what I did during the war and why I had answered her advertisement. I answered her questions as fully and honestly as I could.

'I entertain from time to time,' she said. 'Do you think that you can take this on as well as your other duties, particularly that we still have rationing?' [34]

'The doctor and his wife entertained quite frequently,' I replied. 'I served at cocktail parties and when they had guests for evening meals.'

'I thought so. You seem eminently qualified to me, Mrs Etheridge. When would you be able to start?'

A wave of excitement at her sudden announcement set my heart beating faster.

'Oh, thank you, Mrs Walker. Thank you. I can start just as soon as I find a nursery place for David. I wouldn't be able to look after him as well as do my job here to the best of my ability.'

'Ah, I was coming to that,' she said. 'I hope that you don't mind me observing that your son's eyesight is rather poor.'

'Not at all. He's been wearing glasses for a few months now. I'll also have to find a school that can take him.'

'I imagine that any nursery would be fine,' said Mrs Walker. 'But it will be his first school that would have

---

[34] Food rationing for many commodities continued into the early to mid 1950s.

to be chosen carefully. I happen to know that Birmingham Education has a school for partially sighted children. It has a nursery year and is an infant and junior school as well. You might try there.'

'Thank you, I'm very grateful for your advice,' I said.

I wonder how she knows so much about schools.

'I'll write down the details before you go,' said Mrs Walker. 'I am very glad that you will be coming here to live. Don't worry if you haven't got David into the nursery before you start. We will work things out until he goes.'

Mrs Walker rang a small brass bell that she kept on the table beside her. 'Amanda will show you out,' she said, extending her wrinkled hand. 'Please let me know when you can start.'

'Yes, certainly. I'm staying with my sister in Pritchatts Road.'

'Oh, that's not too far.'

'If you could wait a week or two while I sort a few things out,' I said. 'I will write and give you a date.'

'Very good, Mrs Etheridge. I am looking forward to having you and David here. My grandchildren live nearby. At the moment, they take it in turns to look in on me and do for me.'

David had put the bricks away neatly.

'Come along, son. We're going now.'

My son waved shyly at Mrs Walker.

'Goodbye, little man,' she whispered.

At the open front door, Mrs Walker's granddaughter said: 'We don't mind dropping in, but having someone living-in full time will be a weight off our minds. I'm so glad that you have accepted.'

'Thank you,' I said. 'I am very much looking forward to working for your grandmother. What surprises me though,' I added in a quiet voice, 'is that she is willing to give a home to both of us.'

'Gran is generous is so many ways,' said Amanda. 'The welfare and education of children is very close to her heart. It runs in the family.'

I wonder what can she mean.

'Goodbye for now, Mrs Etheridge.'

'Goodbye,' I replied.

I heard the door close behind us as I held David's hand while we crunched our way down the short drive to the pavement. 'Home now, Mummy,' he said as we set off along Hintelsham Avenue en route to Danny's prefab.

'That house will be our home soon,' I said.

'Will the bricks be there?'

'I hope so, son. I hope so.'

When there were no visitors in the afternoon or when Mrs Walker was not entertaining dinner guests, she devoted an hour each evening between five o'clock and six o'clock to David. They played games, built things and read. She taught David to read by the time he was four, using a box of wooden letters. Mrs Walker did so much to help my son; it was she who encouraged and nurtured his love of books and reading.

Although I didn't earn very much as Mrs Walker's housekeeper, it mattered little. This remarkable woman gave us a home: we had our own bedrooms and a small sitting room to ourselves.

I can still picture David playing endlessly with the box of wooden bricks and re-doing a wonderful jigsaw of the British Isles, each coloured piece the shape of a county: another of Mrs Walker's educational toys.

I secured a place at the George Auden School for Partially Sighted Children shortly after we began living at Number 18 Hintelsham Avenue. Mrs Walker was instrumental in helping me get David into the nursery class in September 1950. This was an important start for David. He had (and still has) serious life-long eyesight problems. Mrs Walker seemed to know who to talk to in the educational world in Birmingham.

The school was two bus rides away from Hintelsham Avenue. A middle-aged woman, Mrs Bird, employed as a volunteer "bus guide" for the school, called for David every morning. They had to walk quite a long distance through the Queen Elizabeth Hospital, then across part of the University of Birmingham campus to Selly Oak to catch a bus to Kings Heath, then another bus to the school on Mosely Road.[35]

Thinking about it now, as I write this, it must have felt a long journey for a three-and-a-half-year-old little boy, beginning the long walk to the first bus and ending the day with the same walk in the reverse direction. It must have taken him and his guide the best part of two hours at either end of the day. Perhaps I didn't worry too much about the inconvenience of the journey at the time. I was grateful that my son was at the right school.

After two years in the nursery, David joined the infants' class at just over the age of five and a half in September 1952.

---

[35] I spent six years as a student at the university I walked across as a little boy.

One morning, towards the end of his first year in the infants, Mrs Bird handed me an envelope when she brought David home. 'See you in the morning, David,' she said cheerily on her way down the short drive.

'Goodbye,' called out my son.

I opened the sealed envelope while David was with Mrs Walker and there was a pause in the business of getting her evening meal prepared. The brief letter enclosed, written by Miss Ludford, the headmistress of George Auden school, assured me that there was nothing to worry about, but that she wanted to see me about a matter of some importance.

What can it be?

Miss Ludford hoped that I would come to school with Mrs Bird the day after tomorrow.

I asked Mrs Walker's permission to have part of the morning in question off to go to David's school after I served her with breakfast. 'Of course, dear. It sounds important.'

'I should be back by lunchtime,' I said.

It was obvious that David and Mrs Bird got on famously. They chatted well-nigh non-stop as they trod their familiar route with me trailing behind. I almost felt ignored and left out were it not for my little boy glancing behind from time to time with a smile on his face.

His glasses need straightening again.

David trotted off to join his class the moment we entered the school premises. Mrs Bird showed me to Miss Ludford's office.

'I'll bring him home, as usual,' said Mrs Bird. 'He's a lovely little boy, Mrs Etheridge,' she added.

'He seems very happy here,' I said.

'It's a good school. I think that you'll like the Head.'

I knocked on the frosted glass of the upper part of the door. 'Come in,' came the response. 'Ah, Mrs Etheridge. Please sit down.'

I must have looked worried.

'It's nothing to worry about. Please don't be concerned. We haven't met, have we. You must have spoken to my deputy just before David started here.'

'Yes.'

'The reason I asked you to come in and see me … well, it's about David's education or his future education to be exact.'

'Yes.'

'Mrs Etheridge, in my opinion David would receive a better education elsewhere.'

'You mean not in the juniors here?'

'I know this must sound rather sudden, but I really do feel that this junior school would not suit David in the long run. Your son is very bright, Mrs Etheridge. You probably know that. His reading age is almost two years ahead of his class.'

That'll be Mrs Walker's doing.

'Where would you recommend he goes next?' I asked. 'He's not been here very long.'

'I know how this must seem and I know that you are probably concerned now that you have heard what I have to say. But my staff and I genuinely feel that David's full potential would be better fulfilled elsewhere. We can offer him a good education until he is eleven. However, Lickey Grange would offer him a better education as a junior, so that he can go on to the secondary school that is linked to Lickey Grange. Pupils transfer from the junior school to the secondary, providing a sound education up to the age of sixteen.

We can't offer a secondary route here. Do you see what I mean?'

'I think so. I haven't given his secondary school much thought. He's only six.'

'I know it seems early to be thinking about post-eleven school for David. However, I am concerned that a special school should be available for him. It would be what he needs.'

'Of course, I realise that he'd need to be at a partially sighted school until he reaches school-leaving age.'

'At least we're agreed on that,' said Miss Ludford.

'What kind of school is Lickey Grange?' I asked.

'Officially, it is a school for the blind.'

'For the blind!'

'Please don't be alarmed. Officially, yes. But there are many partially sighted pupils there. David wouldn't be the only one. The school is highly experienced in teaching a mixture of blind and partially sighted children.'

'Oh, I see. Where is it?'

'It's a boarding school near Bromsgrove. David would have to become a boarder.'

'At such a young age!'

This is all very worrying.

'I know how it must seem, Mrs Etheridge. But I honestly believe that Lickey Grange would be best for your son.'

My mind raced with jumbled thoughts and questions. I worried how a little boy aged six would cope with boarding school.

'I can see how troubled you are, Mrs Etheridge. Would you think about it. There are a few weeks before the summer break when we can set the arrangement in motion, so there's no hurry.'

Miss Ludford stood and extended her right hand in a gesture that suggested that the interview was over.

'I'll think about it,' I said.

'Please come and see me when you have decided one way or another.'

'I will and thank you for seeing me today.'

'Not at all. My pleasure,' said Miss Ludford as she held open the door of her office. 'David is a very bright little boy. We all want the very best for him.'

I'll talk to Mrs Walker.

The two bus journeys from David's school to Selly Oak found me pondering what it would be like for my son to live away from home at a boarding school for the foreseeable future. The long walk from Selly Oak to Hintelsham Avenue didn't result in me coming to a decision.

One thing was clear: it would be easier for me to carry out my considerable duties in Mrs Walker's employ without my son to get ready before school and without trying to look after him as well as carry out my job to the best of my ability. I immediately felt a pang of guilt stab me in the stomach for thinking such a thing.

'I'll miss our afternoons together,' said Mrs Walker that evening after I told her about what Miss Ludford had to say about David's future education.

'I think I'll take her advice,' I said.

'We can carry on with our evenings together when David comes home for the holidays,' said Mrs Walker. 'It does seem rather hard for him to go away from home at such a young age though,' she added.

I tried to hide my sadness at the thought while I cleared away Mrs Walker's supper tray, only to give vent to tears in the kitchen where I couldn't be heard.

All I could think of was my little boy asleep upstairs not knowing what I was letting him in for.

'How will he cope? How on earth will he cope?' I said quietly.

*

I was permitted to collect David every third weekend and bring him home to Mrs Walker's. Taking him back to boarding school after a weekend or at the end of the school holidays was very upsetting for both of us. I doubt that David knew how upset I was on those occasions. I did my best to hide it from him until I started down the long drive between the school buildings and the Bromsgrove to Birmingham Road. Every time I left him to go and catch the bus back to Birmingham, I cried all the way down the seemingly endless drive, waving to the lonely little figure in the distance.

If David was unhappy at his first boarding school, he didn't show it. I don't know if he kept his feelings to himself: he seemed to accept the situation and just got on with it.

Weekends at home and school holidays were a joy to all of us. David often read to Mrs Walker during their evenings together and when the weather was fine he rode around the large rear garden on a three-wheeled cycle that she gave him.

Many is the time I looked out of the kitchen window to see David trundling his little wooden wheelbarrow that I bought for him, following Mrs Walker around the garden gathering deadheads. She suffered badly from arthritis and was unable to bend down to pick them up from the lawn where she had discarded the dead flower heads.

Mrs Walker had an electric mobility chair that she rode on to visit her sister who lived nearby. Hurt, the gardener, would push the chair out of the garage, help Mrs Walker into it and away she would go with David running alongside as the strange-looking black vehicle with its long steering wheel hummed its way down Hintelsham Avenue.

Towards the end of the 1950s, Mrs Walker's arthritis spread throughout her body until she became semi-invalid and bedridden. A live-in nurse joined our small household, as Mrs Walker needed much more care than I was able or qualified to give. Whilst I understood and accepted the necessity of a full-time nurse, her arrival was a very sad day for me as it spelt the end of the close personal contact between me and Mrs Walker; she had become more than my employer: we had become friends. The nurse soon seemed to take over and, in her own words, became "the queen bee".

I made one of the most difficult decisions of my life when I resolved to end my period of employment as Mrs Walker's housekeeper.

David took it very badly when I told him that we were leaving our home. He was inconsolable when I took him back to Lickey Grange after the Easter Holidays.

'Where are we going to live, Mummy?' he asked as we walked up the drive towards the school entrance.

'I don't know yet, son,' I replied. 'I'll find somewhere, and I'll get a new job. In the meantime, I won't be able to collect you for the next home weekend until I've found us somewhere to live.'

David's face crumpled under the weight of this news. He fought back tears that I could see forming behind his glasses.

Be brave, my son. Be brave.

'I'll contact the head and let him know if I can collect you at half-term,' I said as confidently as I could. 'We're here,' I added pointlessly, handing David his suitcase. 'Goodbye, son,' I whispered, holding him tightly to me.

I let go and held my hand against his cheek before starting down the drive, not daring to look back at first. Eventually I turned around, tears clouding my vision. There he stood, hand in the air, still rather than waving, his suitcase at his feet.

A very influential period of my life soon came to an end, a period of stability and happiness. I will always be grateful that Mrs Walker employed me as her housekeeper. The years I spent living in her home helped to dispel some of the bitterness I felt towards the world.

The period between Easter and the summer of 1958 proved to be one of disruption and turmoil in our lives. I left Mrs Walker's employ a few days after Easter. David had gone back to boarding school, so I faced saying goodbye to her on my own.

'Say goodbye to the little man,' said Mrs Walker on the morning I took my leave.

'I will,' I replied, trying not to let my quivering voice give away how emotional I felt.

'Would you hand me the muslin bag on my side table please, Jean.'

I handed her the bag.

'This is for you, a keepsake, something to remember me by. Open it, Jean.'

I drew open the string, put my hand inside the bag and drew out three pieces of what looked like silver.

'They fit together to form a long silver buckle. I would like you to have it.' [36]

I looked from what lay in my hand to Mrs Walker and back again. 'I hardly know what to say, Mrs Walker. Thank you … thank you very much.'

'It was a gift to me. Now I chose to give it to you.'

I put the three pieces of silver carefully in their bag, slipped it into my handbag and made ready to say my final farewell.

'The past few years have been very special for David and for me, Mrs Walker. David and I will never forget you and everything that you have done for us.'

'Goodbye, dear,' she said holding my hand with both of hers, her grip weak, her voice barely audible. 'Goodbye.'

I turned away from her bed for the last time and closed the door of her downstairs bedroom. I saw myself out, not wishing to have to make small talk with the nurse and made my way down Hintelsham Avenue. It felt very strange to be without a job and a home. I set off for my sister's prefab with a heavy heart. At least David was in school and cared for: it was up to me to work out what to do next.

---

[36] My mother gave the silver buckle to my wife. It featured on the BBC's Antiques Roadshow in the Summer of 2021.

This thought rattled around in my head all the way to Danny's. Questions that had no answers swirled around in my mind, helping to suppress my deep sadness at leaving 18 Hintelsham Avenue. I arrived at Danny's and let myself in with a key that she had lent me: both Danny and Tommy were at work.

The silence of the empty prefab folded around me as I sat at the kitchen table, feeling numb and unable to put my mind to anything. I must have sat there for many minutes: my cup of tea was stone cold and I had not taken off my coat.

'C'mon, Jean. Buck up,' I said aloud. 'This won't do.'

I washed my cup, took my coat off and switched the kettle back on.

Mrs Walker really was a very remarkable woman, a woman of consequence in my life.[37]

I stayed with Danny and Tommy while I looked for somewhere to live and gave serious thought to getting a new job. Disruption showed its face to my son: he transferred to Rowton Castle in September, a senior boarding school for the blind, near Shrewsbury, about fifty miles away.

Just after I got David settled into his new school, something happened that fragmented what was left of my unsettled situation, something that would have a profound effect on the rest of my life.

---

[37] Over seventy years on from these events, I occasionally walk past 18 Hintelsham Avenue en route to Harborne High Street from the University of Birmingham railway station.

Chapter Eighteen

Making Our Way in the World

After I left Mrs Walker's employ, I worked behind the counter of a dress shop in nearby Harborne, largely so that I could pay my way living at Danny's while I looked for better paid work. An advertisement in the *Birmingham Post* for telephonists attracted my attention. I applied successfully for the job with what was then known as The Post Office. My two months' period of training began in September.

Danny and Tommy urged me to continue to stay with them, a very kind offer which I declined: they had two boys to look after; three adults and two children would be too many folk living in a prefab. I didn't think that it was fair that they should put me up as well as David when he came home from boarding school during the school holidays.

I found digs at the top of a house in Bournville. Mr and Mrs Hudson, a retired couple, were kindly and welcoming. I shared the bathroom and kitchen with them and there was a tiny loft bedroom that David could use when he was home from school.

My life became settled to some extent while I stayed with the Hudsons. David was away at boarding school and once my training came to an end at the main telephone exchange in Birmingham, I was fortunate enough to be transferred to a smaller exchange in Stirchley, a walkable distance from my digs in Bournville.

I thoroughly enjoyed my training. I had found something that I was good at, something other than domestic work that I seem to have been destined for. I did not want to continue my life as someone else's housekeeper for the rest of my days. I wanted to turn my back on it and seek a new direction. My new job gave me the opportunity to splice together the fragments of my life and make my own way.

'You have a good voice, Jean,' Mrs Walker had said when I told her of my plans during one of my visits soon after I left. 'You have the voice for it. Good luck, dear. And how is the little man getting on at school?'

We visited Mrs Walker from time to time. She always took an interest in David's education and welfare.[38]

David was never far from my thoughts, particularly during the walk to and from work. A pedestrian walkway, known as the Birdcage, took me from Bournville through the Cadbury factory on my way to the telephone exchange. To this day, I can still conjure the strong sweet aroma of chocolate production that hung in the air as I made my way past factory buildings.

If not David, then my thoughts often turned to my dear sister, Danny; she who had done so much for me and David, offering us a home for a while. I was very lucky to have my sister living near me. As I ended the walk through the Birdcage, I imagined Danny sitting at her desk in one of the buildings I passed where she worked as a wages clerk.

Peter, the younger of Danny's two boys, had similar eye conditions to David. Peter boarded at Exhall Grange school, a school near Coventry that catered for

---

[38] I don't remember any of these visits.

visually impaired children.[39] Danny and I often wondered why our boys had similar eyesight problems; no one else in the Muir family seemed to suffer in the same way.

The walk back from work through the Birdcage usually focussed on worrying when I could use the kitchen to make a meal for myself that evening. The shared arrangement just about worked but became strained and increasingly impractical when David came home from boarding school during half-term.

I must find myself a better place to live is a thought that troubled me constantly during the time I lived with the Hudsons.

A week or so after I started work on the switchboard at Stirchley in November, one of the supervisors called me into her office at lunchtime.

'It's nothing to be worried about, Mrs Etheridge,' she said. 'There are some forms for you to sign, now that you are an employee of a government department, including the Official Secrets Act.'

'Oh, that does sound important,' I said.

'Purely routine. We all must sign it. To complete the paperwork, we need to see your birth certificate. It's part of the procedure. We don't keep it. You will get it straight back.'

'I've never been asked for it until now,' I said after a moment's hesitation. 'I don't have it. I don't recall ever seeing it.'

'Perhaps your parents have it?'

---

[39] Whilst George Auden, Lickey Grange and Rowton Castle have gone, Exhall Grange still operates as a special school.

'They must have. I'll find out as soon as I can.'

'No hurry, Mrs Etheridge. If they can't lay their hands on it, you can request a copy.'

'Where from?'

'In your case, Edinburgh.'

She remembered I'm from Scotland.

I wrote to Mother later that evening and posted the letter at the Post Office on Bournville Green on my way to work the following morning. I emphasised the importance of her sending the document and its significance for my employment.

My mother replied by return of post: she was unable to find my birth certificate.

'Have you got yours?' I asked Danny on the following Sunday afternoon when I called in for tea and one of my sister's excellent scones.

'Aye, somewhere. I've no seen it recently though.'

'Mother says she cannae fin mine,' I grumbled. 'I need it for the Post Office.'

'You'd think Davey and Kate would keep all ten in a safe place,' quipped Tommy.

'Aye, ee'd think so,' rejoined Danny.

'I'll have tae send for a replacement,' I said. 'I can't wait for Mother to have another look. She sounded pretty sure in her letter.'

'Did she say onything about Faither?' asked Danny.

'Nothing,' I replied.

'No. How?'

'Ah dinnae ken,' I added.

'Ah heard fri Chrissie yesterday. Faither isn't at all well, Jean.'

'Ah didnae ken,' I said.

'Neither did Ah,' said Danny. 'Not until yesterday, onyway.'

'Why didnae oor mother write us?'

Danny shrugged.

'Well at least we know now,' I said. 'Shall we go up?'

'I can't get any days off this week. It's the end of the month. Our busiest time.'

'I've no been there long,' I said. 'I dinnae like tae ask for leave yet.'

'Try asking for compassionate leave,' suggested Danny.

'We both could,' I added. 'Let's go up the weekend after next. Can ee get the first Friday of December off?'

'Aye, I'll try,' said Danny. 'We can go up on the Friday and come back on the Sunday. We'll only have tae ask for yin day off.'

'A long drive,' said Tommy.

'We've nae choice,' said Danny.

'I'll get the car checked over and fill it up on the way home on the Thursday. It'll be ready for you to leave early the next morning.'

'If we can get the Friday off, come and stay here on the Thursday,' suggested my sister. 'Pack an overnight bag. We'll leave in the dark if we have tae.'

I called in at the supervisor's office at lunchtime on Monday.

'I'll find the address for you,' she said, 'and bring it to your position. We've had this sort of thing in the past. I'll just have to find the correct name and job title in Edinburgh. They are likely to send you a form to fill in, but at the end of the process they'll send you a copy of your birth certificate.'

I thanked Mrs Davidson and returned to my position on the switchboard.

Later that afternoon, Mrs Davidson placed an envelope in front of me. 'It's all in there,' she whispered.

I nodded by way of thanks, while I took a call for a number in London.

I wrote to Edinburgh that evening, explaining the situation, giving them my date and place of birth.

'I assume that I was born in Dumfries Maternity,' I said to Danny as we motored along the Birmingham to Wolverhampton Road in the dark.

'And they say they can't find you,' said Danny.

'No record,' I replied.

Danny glanced briefly at me, then turned back to face forward, her frown and her voice reflecting puzzlement. 'Whit's garn on? There must be an explanation. Bureaucracy eh!'

'Ah'll hae tae pester Ma. Ah dinnae like tae, what wi Pa poorly. But ma new job depends on it. Ah might lose it if Ah can't get this sorted out.'

'Ah'm sure there's got tae be an explanation, Jean. Let's see what Ma says. We did the right thing asking for compassionate leave. Your supervisor sounds okay.'

'She is that. And your boss.'

'We'll see what's what at hame and come back on Sunday,' said Danny.

'Should be long enough to see how serious Pa is. Whether Ma needs any help,' I said.

'She should be okay with Betty over the road and Angus down the road.[40]

---

[40] Two of my mother's younger siblings.

'The men are nae much yiss in these situations,' I suggested. 'It'll be left tae us sisters, just you see. Ma is going to need her daughters to rally round.'

'Aye, and Davie can be difficult,' muttered Danny.[41] 'Thank goodness it's getting light.'

'Wull ma faither want onything, Ma?' asked Danny after we finished tea.

'He's no much of an appetite the noo,' replied Ma. 'Ah gave him some soup afore ee got here. He sleeps an awfy lot.'

Danny frowned. 'When's the doctor coming in next?'

'He said he'll pop in first thing Monday,' said Ma.

'Guid. And ee'll write us wi ony news, Ma.'

'Aye,' she replied.

Danny, Ma, and I sat in the living room of Number 2 Ashgrove Crescent, warmed by a roaring coal fire, deep in thought. All of us worried about Pa's health to the extent that we thought of little else, suspending conversation and any further questions about him.

The entrance of my eldest brother, Davie, broke the silence. 'The back's open, so Ah came straight in. Danny. Jean.'

'Davie,' we replied.

'How's Pa?' he asked.

'Much the same,' replied Ma.

'How lang are ee up?'

''Till the moran's moran,' replied Danny.

'Have ee a cup, Ma?'

Mother went into the kitchen.

---

[41] Davie, Jean's older brother, lived in Lockerbie at the time.

Davie leant forward in the dining chair he had occupied the moment he walked in and whispered: 'It's serious. Ah dinnae think Ma realises. We need tae prepare fi the worst.'

'She kens,' said Danny.

'Aye. Doctor Buchannan telt iss last week that there's little hope. Ah didnae tell Ma, though,' said Davie.

Mother came in and handed Davie a cup of tea. 'Thanks, Ma.'

'While Ah think of it, did ee fin ma birth certificate, Ma?'

'Ah've telt ee, Ah havenae,' she replied, her voice rising with a note of irritation.

'Ah tried tae get a replacement fri Edinburgh, but they cannae fin iss in their records. Ah really need it, Ma. Ah could lose ma job if Ah dinnae produce it.'

My clumsy attempt to take my mother's mind off things only served to make her angry, a reaction that took me by surprise.

'Ah'm very sorry, Ma. Ah could help ee look fi it. My job depends—'

'Why d'ye need it?' asked Davie.

'Ah'll lose ma new job if they dinnae see it. It's something tae do wi government regulations, Davie.'

'Ye chose a fine time tae ask fi it,' he snapped.

'Ah'm sorry. It's just that while we're here—'

'Ye heard Ma.'

'Aye, and Ah've tried to get a replacement, but they cannae fin iss.'

'What did ee tell 'em?'

'Ma date of birth and that Ah wis born in Dumfries Maternity,' I said, glancing at my mother.

She made no reply.

'They're looking in the wrong place,' said Davie.

'What d'ye mean?'

'Shall Ah tell her or wull you, Mother,' said Davie.

My mother shook her head, wringing her hands in her lap while weeping quietly.

'Ah wull then,' announced my brother, turning to face me. 'It's nae wonder they cannae fin ee. Ye wusnae born in Dumfries.'

'Where then? Home, at home in the Fechan?'

'No, Jean. Ee were born in Glasgow.'

'Glasgow!'

'Aye, Glasgow.'

'How duv ee ken?' interrupted Danny in a calm voice.

'Ah just ken,' replied Davie. 'Well, Ma. Am Ah reet?'

My mother's weeping turned into loud sobs.

'Whit's mair, the man upstairs dying in his bed isnae yer faither.'

My mother's sobs grew even louder and more frequent, shaking her whole body. I looked from my brother to my mother, then at my sister. No one said anything.

'What do you mean?' I demanded loudly. 'I don't understand any of this.'

'It's why they cannae fin ee, Jean,' repeated Davie. 'Ye had tae know some day. Ye did ask, so Ah telt ee.'

'Ma?' I said, my voice choking.

My mother nodded, very slowly, still sobbing and gasping for each intake of breath.

'Yer secret's oot, Ma,' said Davie. 'It had tae come oot eventually. Better now than—'

'Enough! That's enough,' said Danny in a commanding voice.

'Ah wis only trying tae—'

'Tae WHIT?' shouted Danny. 'Upset everyone. Wull, ee've din that a'reet. Ee should garn reet noo.'

My brother didn't dare argue with his sister. 'Ah'll call the moran,' he said to our mother on his way out of the room. Danny followed him; I heard raised voices outside the back door.

I wonder what's being said.

'Ah'm going up,' I said to Ma.

I stood at the foot of the stairs, relieved to be on my own. I held on to the lower banister: I felt dizzy and nauseous; holding on to something helped to stop the feeling that the empty, dark hallway of my parents' house was swirling about me. I held my throat with my free hand until the feeling of suffocation eased sufficiently for me to climb the stairs slowly and open my father's bedroom door.

'Aye, it's Jeanie,' said my father in a weak voice.

I sat on the edge of the bed and looked at the face of the man who I had called "faither" for the past forty years.

'Pa, are ee a'reet?'

'Aye, Jeanie Ma's looking efter iss just fine. Ah dinnae want tae garn tae the hospital. Ah'm better off at hame.'

'Lean forward. Yer pillows need sorting.'

My father had lost weight since I saw him last. He was hardly any weight to hold while I adjusted his pillows. He gripped my hand as he lay back. 'Ah heard voices, raised voices. Whit's garn on, Jean?'

'Something Davie said about iss.'

'Aye. Ah can guess.'

'Why didnae ee tell iss?'

My father looked at me without answering at first. His kind eyes fixed on my tear-filled eyes. 'We thought that it wid be easier just tae carry on as if Ah wis yer faither. Dinnae be angry with yer Ma, wull ee Jean,' he added suddenly.

'Of course not.'

'We decided tae carry on as a family when Ah got back fri the war and fun that ee'd arrived. Ah wanted ee as ma daughter too.'

I could barely see my father's face through my tears.

'Ee wull a'wis be oor daughter, Jean.'

'And ee wull a'wis be ma faither.'

'We kept oor secret for over forty years.'

'Whi else knew?'

'I'll tell ee yin day.'

'And Ah want tae fin oot whit happened tae ye and Ma during the war,' I added. 'How Ah came along.'

'Aye, yin day. Ee should be telt.'

I clasped my arms around my father's neck and held him as tightly as I dared.

'Oor daughter … oor daughter,' he whispered as I held him.

'Ah'm away doon noo,' I said as I relaxed my embrace. 'Danny's wi is. Wull Ah send her up?'

'Aye.'

'Ah'll see ee later, Pa,' I said, turning at his bedroom door.

A single tear rolled down the cheek of my dear father. I closed the door, took a deep breath, went downstairs and stood outside the living room door for a few moments, staring at the upper panel. A few minutes earlier in this very room, an exchange of words had changed who I was. That's all it took: just a few words; a revelation that lay heavily on the surface of my mind. I had been told something that somehow had been kept secret from me until now, today, in this very room, a secret that lay hidden for over forty years, revealed in no more than a few seconds.

It would take a long time for what I now knew to penetrate my troubled mind.

I could hear voices behind the door: my mother and my sister were in quiet conversation. I turned the doorknob; Danny and Ma stopped what they were saying and looked towards me. I resisted the urge to ask my mother why she didn't tell me.

Why didn't you tell me?

It repeated over and over in my head, but that's where it stayed, unsaid, lingering and held back in a blur of questions.

A fog of dismay fell upon me that day, casting a shadow on my childhood and a blight on my identity, awakening the pain of disappointment as it visited my life once again.

I wrote to Edinburgh again, filled in another form and awaited the response: a copy of my birth certificate duly arrived.

I took the long brown envelope with me to work and, despite the chill of a January morning, opened it while I sat on a bench on Bournville Green.

The typed facsimile of my birth certificate showed my mother's maiden name – she hadn't used the name "Muir" – and my first name with the surname "McDermott", evidently the name of my natural father.

I re-read the document several times. It posed yet more questions: why did the name Muir not appear and who was Thomas McDermott? My date of birth was shown as 16th September 1917. I always celebrated my birthday on the 15th. Changing the date of my birthday seemed minor compared to the enormity of what the document that I held in my hand represented.

I hoped that passers-by hadn't noticed me drying my eyes before I replaced the document in its envelope and slid it into my handbag.

What if the Post Office hadn't asked?

I set off for the entrance to the Birdcage. That day I walked to work as a different person, with a new maiden name and a different birthday. I would still be known as Mrs Jean Etheridge; I didn't think that anyone at work would be interested in my name at birth. I would hand over my birth certificate, secure my job and perhaps my future with the Post Office.

I quickened my pace, eager to take my place at the switchboard. Connecting callers to their destinations would occupy my mind, pushing the events of my recent visit home to one side.

I felt a new determination overtake the revelation thrust upon me as to my identity and that of my natural father. In my heart, I remained Jean Muir, officially Jean Etheridge, and David Muir would always be my father.[42] Nothing, not even my birth certificate, would change that. Even if the truth of my brother's revelation became widely known, I would ignore any questions or questioning looks from folks in the Fechan.

I vowed to remember what my father said to me as he lay dying, remember it and hold on to it until the end of my days.

---

[42] After her divorce in 1956, my mother kept her married name for the remainder of her life.

My father remained bedridden for the next few weeks, looked after by my mother until his passing on 31st January 1959. David took the news of his grandfather's death very badly, which was of no surprise to me. My father always made a fuss of him when Danny, Tommy, and their boys took David with them to the Fechan for summer holidays during the 1950s. I usually journeyed by coach: there wasn't enough room in their car for another adult.

I wrote to David to let him know that his grandfather's funeral would be on Thursday 12th February. David had attended Rowton Castle for just over a term; I thought it best not to take him out of school on the occasion of the funeral. In the event, David didn't express a wish to attend. Perhaps at the age of twelve, he didn't feel ready to attend a funeral: it would have been his first.

As I write this part of my memoir, I can remember the scene of my mother and her nine children gathered around the grave of my father.[43] My brothers and sisters had arrived at the Fechan from all corners of the United Kingdom, leaving their distant lives for a few days to mourn Father.

I had no idea if anyone else, apart from Danny and me, were aware what my brother knew. My siblings seemed to treat me as their sister as if nothing had changed. We mourned as equals: only my brother Davie showed distance in his manner to me.

---

[43] My mother's sister Kathy died in 1950.

We stood at the graveside exchanging brief glances whilst listening to the vicar say the last prayers, until our gaze was drawn to the deep hole that embraced Father's coffin. I stepped forward and took my turn to drop a handful of earth onto the lid of the wooden box that lay below me.

Prior to the funeral service, I lingered at the door of the church, where a wedding group had assembled sixteen years earlier, my husband and me in the centre, my mother and father nearby to my left. Now my father has gone and my mother is alone with no husband or any of my siblings living with her.

I looked across at my mother, consoled by Aunty Chrissie. The sound of her weeping pricked my eyes. I worried how she would cope with loneliness.

I too felt rather lonely as the Muir family walked silently towards the gate of the graveyard that led to the Hoddom to Ecclefechan Road.

'Goodbye, Father,' I said quietly, as I too left the graveside and caught up with the others.

Standing on the very place where my wedding photograph had been taken soon sent my thoughts to my son as I sat in the rear seat of Danny and Tommy's car on the way back to the Fechan after the funeral service. I had just lost my father: David never knew his. I wondered what my son would be doing on a cold February morning and I worried about how he was coping with his new boarding school. He was allowed only one weekend visit home during term-time; it would soon be half-term and I had no home to offer him. My new job was safe; my next task would be to find a home for us. As soon as I got back to Birmingham, I resolved to double my efforts to find somewhere to live.

*

My son boarded from age six to age nineteen. It was a blessing in a way. It was several years until I found a proper home to offer him when he came home during the school holidays. He never complained about our accommodation; he understood my circumstances.

During his early years as a boarder, two of our "homes" had a shared bathroom and toilet. Towards the end of his schooling, I finally managed to rent a flat with two bedrooms: a proper home where my son could spend his school holidays.

It soon became obvious that my son was bright and, despite Miss Ludford's advice, he would not develop his full potential at a school for the blind. I failed to see the point of him learning how to read and write Braille when he could read and write normally. I fretted that I had made a mistake in following her advice in the first place.

I took a chance and managed to get David transferred to a "normal" secondary school, a boarding school in Stourbridge, a town about fifteen miles from Birmingham, a distance too far for him to attend as a "day boy" and live at home.[44] David entered the Third Year at Old Swinford in 1962.

David achieved very good GSE O and A level results at Old Swinford, which enabled him to attend the University of Birmingham in 1966, where he gained a B.Sc. in 1969 and a Ph.D. three years later.

---

[44] I don't know if my mother tried to get me into a school where I could attend daily.

I am very proud of what my son achieved at university. I am certain that Mrs Walker would have been delighted, as would my father.

David didn't leave home until he embarked upon his Ph.D. I was very upset and cried when he told me that he was leaving home to live with a group of friends who were also studying for their doctorate degrees.

Looking back on the years following my father's death at the age of seventy-two up to the time that David left home, I feel very glad that David was able to have his own space in our flat when he came home from Old Swinford during the school holidays. The years of struggling to find a decent flat after moving around from one temporary home to another paid off. I also feel very fortunate that David kept me company while he studied for his first degree, but I had to accept that he would leave me eventually. Perhaps David wanted to stay at home for a while after spending a total of thirteen years at three boarding schools.

It was while David was living away from home studying for his Ph.D. that he met a nice girl called Annette. They married in July 1973, a very happy day for me, a day that helped to make up for some of the unhappiness of my life.

After they were married, David left home for good to begin a new life with Annette. Again, I feel fortunate that they lived in Birmingham, not far from me.

Up to that point, I had not told David about his natural grandfather. I wondered if he would find out one day, just as I had made a discovery about my natural father, or whether I should reveal our family secret to him.

Chapter Nineteen

Retirement

I took early retirement from British Telecom (formerly The Post Office) in 1975. My health was rather poor, so I took the redundancy package that was on offer.

Retirement was not what I imagined it to be. Perhaps I felt that way because I was on my own. When you share retirement with a partner, it might be different.

I always had it in mind that I would have my mother live with me when I retired so that I could look after her. This was not to be as, in the first instance, my health would not allow it. Now, in 1979, she is a confused old lady of eighty-five and in a hospital for the mentally ill.

The previous year, I travelled up to Ecclefechan and looked after her for a month. To begin with she was in a terrible state, physically and mentally; she was also undernourished. After a few days under my care, she improved until she looked altogether a different person. It soon became clear that she needed twenty-four-hour care, too demanding for me to cope on my own.

When I told my elder brother, Davie, who lives only six miles away in Lockerbie, that I was returning home, he did not have a good word to say to me. He had expected me to take on the task of caring for Mother on my own indefinitely. He told others in our family that I had walked out on Mother and that I didn't care about her. This was not true: a healthy person would not have been able to cope, let alone a daughter in poor health herself.

I offered to take turns looking after Mother with my brothers and sister. No one volunteered to help, except for my sister Danny.[45]

My brother's actions had broken all communication with some members of the Muir family. There was one occasion when two of my younger brothers came over from Canada to visit family; they did not call on me.[46]

The predicament with my mother was solely the making of my brother – he created bad blood in the family. Eventually, Davie arranged for Mother to be admitted to hospital and gave up her home.

I telephoned the hospital regularly. The staff told me that my mother was very confused and didn't know where she was.

I visited Mother when I could, once with Danny and Tommy. She was always pleased to see me, even though she seemed bewildered. On one occasion, she asked me if she would end her days in the hospital. It was very distressing to know that my mother had lost her independence and had also lost her mind. She had her own mother on her mind a great deal during my visits and wept when she told me that her mother was dead.

The situation made me feel very despondent, provoking the familiar unhappy feeling that visited me from time to time like a passing wind as I moved from

[45] My mother's elder sister, Marion, died in 1976, her sister Betty in 1966 and Kathy in 1950.

[46] I can still see my mother crying while I sat with her in her living room. At the time, I couldn't understand why her brothers had not visited her.

place to place, carrying a burden of bitterness and self-doubt. It took an elderly lady, Mrs Walker, to draw its sting shortly after the Second World War; now the death of my mother and isolation from my brothers re-ignited feelings of disquiet and self-questioning:

Has my life fallen between the cracks of where it should have been?

Why didn't I live up to Harry's expectations?

Just who are my family?

The past may never die, but I have tried to leave it behind, render it untouched and less thought of.

Old age coming on as it did for my mother was very sad to see. She had to work so hard to bring up ten children; I wonder how she ever managed.

My mother used to say: "A woman is not fully developed until she becomes a mother."

I do think that there is truth in that.

*

My mother's memoir ends abruptly at this point in 1980, leaving an incomplete story arc without further mention of the occasion of her mother's passing or attending her funeral a year later.

Her memoir began with questions that she posed in its *Introduction*; it ends with questions that she dwelt upon in the main body of the memoir, questions that expose her deepest and profound fears and anxieties that followed her throughout her life, revealing things that she never told me about, things that I never asked about. I decided to include these questions at the end of my interpretation of her memoir in an attempt to revisit her mood of reflection expressed in the Introduction and close it with my mother contemplating her past, returning cyclically from the end of her memoir to its beginning.

In the years that followed the end of her memoir, my Aunty Danny and Uncle Tommy moved back to Scotland to live in Dumfries, a town about twenty miles from Ecclefechan. My mother visited Danny and Tommy annually for several years. Annette and I took my mother to the railway station in Birmingham, furnished her with a First-Class Return ticket and saw her safely and comfortably on her way.

Eventually, as her health deteriorated, my mother's visits to Dumfries came to an end and the responsibility of caring for her fell to me, just as she had tried to do for her mother.

My mother passed away in 2013 at the grand old age of ninety-five. She did not add to her memoir during the thirty-three years that she lived since she made the final entry.

Reflections on a Life

Testament to Fortitude

Father to the Child: Mother to the Son

'I don't know who I am anymore.' My mother's profound declaration echoes in me still.

My mother and I looked at one another, staring into the past, neither of us asking about it.

I was rendered speechless by the sudden expression of her feelings, unable to reply for a while, shocked into silence by its enormity. We had been talking about my plan to write the story of her father, David Muir.[47]

The extant dated copy of my mother's birth certificate shows that she had known for at least fifty years that Thomas McDermott was her natural father, yet our brief discussion that day brought out her anxiety about her past in a way that I had not heard before.

'He remains something of a mystery, Mum,' I said. 'All my efforts and that of a professional genealogist have drawn a blank. Sorry, Mum.'

My mother did not reply.

'Thomas McDermott may well have been a common enough name. There's nothing I can tell you about him, Mum, apart from what is on your birth certificate.'

I cannot remember when my mother showed me her birth certificate, neither can I remember how I felt when I read it.

There remains a kind of repeating symmetry: my mother did not know anything about her natural father; I did not know anything about mine.

---

[47] His story is told in *There Was A Soldier*.

*

In her memoir my mother merely mentions that she was born in Glasgow in 1917 and not in Ecclefechan as she had believed for the first forty years of her life. She states this revelation without comment. How she reacted to the truth: she kept to herself. The things she kept to herself, she also kept from her son.

It is clearly evident that David and Katherine Muir (and others?) kept the contents of my mother's birth certificate a secret until she discovered the truth when she was well into adulthood. If any of her siblings knew or any other members of the Muir family or anyone else in Ecclefechan for that matter knew, then they too did not reveal the identity of her natural father or divulge that David Muir was not her father, a revelation that must have come as a deep and intense shock to my mother.

I will never know how the truth was kept secret for forty years.

Answers to questions that linger with me are buried in Muir family lore: there is no one left alive to answer them. Seven more siblings followed the birth of my mother. They are all out of reach now.

Despite the unknowns lost to family history, I cannot help but draw a single, far-reaching conclusion: David Muir accepted my mother into his family when he returned to Ecclefechan in December 1918, following his release as a prisoner of war at the end of the First World War. I believe unreservedly that David Muir was artless in his genuine fatherhood to my mother. Perhaps the secret that was kept for forty years was hidden to protect her.

My mother always regarded David Muir as her father, just as I always regarded him as my grandfather. These are truths that I will always hold on to.

There are aspects of my mother's life that forged her personality and character that, perhaps, have not emerged from my rendering of her memoir. Her early life experiences probably explain her resilience, toughness and fierce independence in her later life. Pivotal moments of the century that she lived in laid the foundations of the story of her life, determined by events and circumstances: childhood poverty; the Second World War; marriage, then abandonment and motherhood.

Her toughness enabled her to battle against poor health for most of her adult life, one symptom of which were respiratory problems that were likely to be rooted in the working conditions of her war work. Our nephew, Simon, said to me once: 'Aunty Jean is tough isn't she, Uncle David,' after she recovered from another TIA.[48] 'They should put her in goal for the Villa; nothing would get past her.' [49]

I firmly believe that my mother's willpower and determination helped her to recover from breast cancer in the early 1980s.

My mother's independence was legendary. There was the occasion when my wife and I were on holiday in the Yorkshire Dales. I telephoned her early in the week and again later that week; during both conversations she said that she was fine. It was only

[48] A transient ischaemic attack (TIA) is a "mini stroke".
[49] Aston Villa is a Premier League football team in England.

when we returned home at the end of the week that we discovered that she had been in hospital in the period between the two phone calls. 'I didn't want to worry you,' she told us. This scenario played out several times when we were on holiday. On these occasions my mother's neighbour, Doris, accompanied her to hospital.

My mother's toughness and fighting spirit were with her even at the end. When paramedics arrived at her apartment to take her to the hospital after she had a fall, one of them told her: 'Jean, you're having a heart attack!' 'No I'm not,' came the defiant reply. My mother knew her own mind, even at the last. My wife and I were on holiday on the occasion of her last emergency dash to hospital: Doris accompanied her once more.

Doris was much more than a neighbour to my mother; she was a good friend and a staunch source of emotional and practical support. My wife and I could not have managed without Doris.

I believe that my mother thought that she would never achieve good health; she never did, but she reached the age of ninety-five, passing away a month prior to her ninety-sixth birthday.

My mother's inner, emotional self, how she felt to be alone, is now out of reach as it was in life. I didn't ask her about any of these things. Perhaps mothers and sons don't communicate the intimate, deep details of their lives: we didn't. Now, in death, after adapting her memoir, I can begin to understand her early life of poverty and her blossoming in a professional career in her late adulthood. My mother's life, parts of which were shrouded in secrecy, came into focus upon reading her memoir for the first time.

At some point in her working life, my mother must have thought that work had more to offer her than employment as a housekeeper. She retired from British Telecom after several years employed as an instructor; she had discovered her ability to teach. From a housekeeper in other people's homes to an instructor in one of the United Kingdom's largest telecommunications companies: I am immensely proud of what she achieved.

I also greatly admire my mother's charity and voluntary work, which she did not write about in her memoir apart from a very brief mention that she was in charge of the under-fives at a local Sunday school while she was in Mrs Walker's employ. This kind of voluntary work reveals a side of my mother's character that resurfaced during her long retirement when she spent time working for the Women's Royal Voluntary Service (WRVS), carrying out voluntary work in a maternity hospital in Moseley (in Birmingham).

Another charitable activity involved making dolls clothing, purchasing dolls for them and sending them to deprived children as part of a Christmas box of gifts.[50]

Determination was another of my mother's attributes. I am the product of her determination to help me as well as herself, her determination to get me educated in a 'normal' school, her resolve to find and make a home for us. Her tenacity set me on a different path than would have been the case if I had completed

---

[50] One of these dolls left behind in my mother's apartment lives in our house. I pass it several times a day and think of her.

my education in schools for the blind and visually impaired. My mother gave me a sense of who I am, where I came from; she shaped my life. Her life was tarnished by sadness, bitterness, and enduring ill-health. Yet, she gave me life and love, and she fought for me to be well-educated in the face of formidable obstacles.

If it were not for the determination of my mother in securing my education, I would not have written this book or any of my previous books for that matter.

I will always regret and feel guilty about not asking how my mother really felt, felt to be alone, felt to be unwell for years. She kept these things to herself and I didn't ask; I took her for granted. In writing her story, I hope that I have atoned for my shortcomings and have celebrated her life and what she did for me. I dearly wish that I had asked, listened, known, helped her instead of looking to my own life. I wish that I had been more sympathetic and caring. I hope that she would forgive me. I love her and miss her still.

My mother fought for me, fought for my education, fought for somewhere decent for us to live. My abiding wish is that she could have had a happier life, instead of one plagued by poor health and struggle.

When we are gone, we leave behind our stories. I took on the responsibility to tell my part of the Muir family story, make it my duty to tell the stories of David, Kate, and Jean before mine too fades into the past. I know what they did, but not what they thought – that has been left to me to be free with expressing their thoughts and surmise their feelings.

And so, my task is complete. It is time to let go and give leave to my family's story to find its place in the myriad of recorded memory. It's letting go has given me a sense of space and release, a lightness of being, an acute admission of gladness and deep gratitude to David, Kate, and Jean Muir.

I have told their stories because they matter to me, matter more to me now that their telling is over, more than I realised at the outset when I longed to seek answers from those departed. Questions remain unanswered, remain hidden and will always be concealed from view.

It is how the stories are told that matters, that they find a place in a world of family stories and achieve a modicum of permanence.

Telling the story of my grandfather and grandmother in *There Was A Soldier* and my mother's story here, relating their courage and their fortitude against a backdrop of a world at war and social and financial hardship helped me to appreciate where I came from and understand how their stories played into mine.

I feel the weight of privilege having told their remarkable stories in these two books; I hope that I have told their stories well.

Item 5 of my mother's will reads as follows:

I desire that my body will be cremated and my ashes buried with my parents in Hoddom Churchyard, Ecclefechan, Dumfriesshire, Scotland.

The ties that bind are expressed in that wish. My mother's readiness to go home and join her mother and the man she knew as her father was left for me to fulfil.

I end this reflection of my mother's life with a gratifying fragment, one that surfaces in my mind from time to time to bring me joy and a reminder of her achievements. While she was employed as a telephonist, my mother was shortlisted for the voice of the "speaking clock". This is a service provided by British Telecom to this day. Dialling 123 results in a human voice telling the time to the nearest ten seconds. She didn't win, but I feel immensely proud that her voice was good enough to be considered.

It would have been wonderful had she won. I could have listened to my mother telling me the time until another voice was chosen by British Telecom.

'At the third stroke, the time will be …' said Jean Etheridge.

Epilogue

Turn Again Home

We always cheered when we crossed the border between England and Scotland. My mother usually made the journey by long-distance coach; there was never room for her in my Uncle Tommy's car for our annual trip from Birmingham to Ecclefechan. My two cousins, Victor and Peter, my Aunty Danny and Uncle Tommy, and me and our luggage took up all the available space in what were, in those far off days of childhood in the 1950s, small cars by today's standards.

Before the construction of bypasses and, later, the M6 motorway, the route to Scotland wound its way from town to town like a giant piece of rope with a knot for every thirty miles or so.

Us children would audibly tick off the towns as we passed through, eager to put them behind us on the long journey north: Wolverhampton, Stafford, Newcastle-under-Lyme, and Crew. Then came the 'Ws': Widness, Warrington, and Wigan before Preston and Lancaster pointed the way over Shap Fell and on towards Carlisle and the border, where we let Scotland know that we were home at last, after a journey that could take up to twelve hours.

When we arrived at my grandparents' house in Ecclefechan, a remarkable thing happened: my mother and her sister, Danny, found and switched on their Scottish accents almost immediately and didn't let go of them for the whole of the holiday. Us children hadn't learnt how to do this, which meant that we got a lot of bother from the local children who made fun of our Brummie accents.

I am certain that data will show that the weather during the summers in the south of Scotland in the late 1950s and early 1960s was always warm and sunny. It never rained; the sun always shone; we were always outside. There were fields to trespass upon, woods to explore, and every summer we made a den near the watercourse in the nearby glen.

We taught ourselves how to fish with our hands. When we had guddled enough trout, we would gather up our silver treasure from the bank of the stream and take it home for our tea.[51]

My grandparents' house was an end semi-detached council property at the top of the hill leading from the north end of the High Street. Its end position meant that my grandparents had an extra piece of garden to one side. This large plot was entirely given over to growing vegetables. This was just as well, as there were often eight sitting down to evening meals, sometimes as many as ten or twelve members of the Muir family.

When the mysterious uplands of our teenage years beckoned, the frequency of the annual holiday to Ecclefechan dwindled and eventually ceased altogether. Attending university, getting married and working for a living sealed my absence from the Fechan.

On the occasion of my return, my wife is driving us to Scotland. The knots have disappeared from the route where the M6 motorway powers its way north. I need not have doubted how we would detect the border: a

---

[51] Guddling involves groping for fish beneath stones on the bed of a stream, letting each fish rest in the palm of the hand and flipping them out of the water onto the bank.

250

huge Saltire at the side of the carriageway welcomes us to Scotland.

'We're nearly there, Mum,' I tell her.

We park opposite the Ecclefechan Hotel and I get out of the car and look about me. I feel almost weightless, giddy with anticipation and excitement. It is almost fifty years since my previous visit. Half a century of absence eclipsed in an instant. I stand in the entrance of the hotel, look across the wide street to where my grandparents lived one hundred years ago.

Soon we are up the hill to the end house. In my mind's eye, there's my grandmother lifting tatties; there's my fierce Aunty Betty yelling for my cousin Brian to come in for his tea. There are no children playing out in the street though, just a distant echo of shrill voices from a long time ago.

Back in the High Street, the village shop is still there. A young American is behind the counter. Milwaukee, Wisconsin, the United States of America, to Ecclefechan, Dumfries and Galloway, Scotland. There is no time to ask him how the change of address came about: we have an appointment to keep.

The church at Hoddom is a ruin now. I stop and look briefly at the archway where my mother's wedding group assembled for a photograph. It is barely recognisable, merely a part of the shell of this abandoned place of worship.

We pass by the arch on our way to the graveyard that the local council takes good care of. The Muir plot is easily identified by the neat, straight-sided rectangular hole in the earth made by a council worker. My mother's varnished and surpassingly heavy casket of ashes fits perfectly.

'You're home, Mum,' I tell her.

The director of the funeral parlour, resplendent in full Scottish dress, reads a funereal poem: *What is a Mum?*

I read the names of my grandparents on the headstone:

David Muir died 31st January 1959 aged 72
Catherine Johnstone died 27th May 1981 aged 87

and mentally complete the work that I have asked the stonemason to do. A wedge stone will be placed above the place where my mother's casket is buried.

I decided to use the name Johnstone, the family name of my grandmother's mother, on my mother's wedge stone just as her mother's name is recorded.

The wedge stone will read:

IN MEMORIAM
JEAN BURNIE JOHNSTONE
16th SEPTEMBER 1917
17th AUGUST 2013
DAUGHTER OF
CATHERINE AND DAVID MUIR

And so, my mother has shaken the dust of England off her feet and returned to Scotland; she has completed her last journey: the journey home.

My wife and I visit Hoddom churchyard every summer or autumn. We wash the headstone and my mother's wedge stone as well as the headstone of her sister, Diana, and her husband, my Uncle Tommy, whose grave is immediately to the left of my mother's. We change the artificial flowers and trim the grass around the wedge stone and from the foot of each headstone.

I am standing by the Muir plots now, as I mull over how I will end the stories of David, Kate, and Jean.

It is a late September morning. The churchyard is deserted save for Annette and me. A gentle breeze disturbs the tranquillity of the rural setting of the ruined church and its well-kept graveyard.

The peaceful setting draws me to look down at my mother's wedge stone and think about her in life. I picture her as a toddler in the arms of her mother or father. I see her as a young girl, carrying milk pails suspended from a wooden yoke across her slender shoulders. I imagine her standing over a noisy lathe while she undertook war work. Most of all, I recall her independent spirit and her socialist principles. These qualities and her resilience helped her to overcome a lifetime branded with financial struggle and a constant battle with ill-health.

My mother gave me love enough for two in the absence of my father. She brought me up in the shadow of the difficulties faced by a single mother and she made sure that I was well-educated despite my eye conditions. The gratitude I owe to my mother for doing what she did for me is immeasurable.

I make no apology for stating a well-used adage: I owe everything to my mother. She gave me life, love, and a path to follow.

The motto of the Muir clan reads:
Durum patientia frango
which translates as:
By patience, I break what is hard

The motto readily applies to David and Kate, who overcame difficulties and "broke what is hard" by more than merely patience. I have told the story of my grandparents in *There Was A Soldier*. On slivers of fate and interlocking events, my very existence depended. My family might have had an alternative history that excluded me. *There Was A Soldier* is a tribute to my grandparents.

The motto more than fittingly describes my mother. She gave me the gift of life with the odds stacked against her. What can I give in return? Is the telling of her story in this book enough, sufficient to express admiration, respect, love and gratitude? Perhaps … I would like to think so.

This story is my tribute to her.

We leave the churchyard after a long period of contemplation.

'See you next year, Mum,' I tell her as we close the iron gate, step into the lane and begin our journey home.

My mother, Jean, and five of her siblings

Jean is standing top left, aged ten or eleven. Marion is seated with Davie standing behind her

My mother in her eighties

E ♔ R

SUPPLIED FOR THE PUBLIC SERVICE

S.O. BOOK 321

(88 PAGES)

Code 28-321

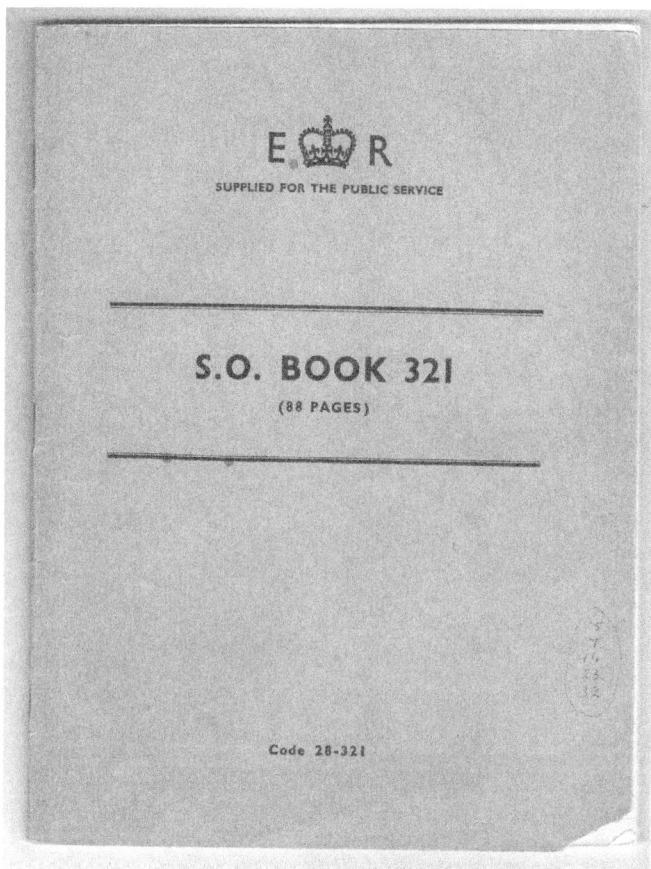

The front cover of my mother's memoir

Coda

Commentary on the Memoir

My approach to turning my mother's memoir into a narrative might be described as "creative non-fiction", giving me the space and scope for speculative imagination to trace the arc of her life.[52] In doing so, I have tried to write scenes, dialogue and my mother's thoughts in the way and style that she would have written them.

There are gaps and omissions in her memoir; some of these lacunae correspond to things relating to her brief marriage, and to her mother and father that she didn't tell me: she kept these thoughts and matters to herself and didn't write about them.

My mother's brief memoir lies on my desk as I write this coda. The forty sides of writing in her HMSO notebook give a deep insight into her childhood and the poverty that her family experienced; a level of poverty that seems unthinkable today. Apart from dialogue, there was little that I needed to add to this section.

Similarly, my mother's descriptions of working away from home after leaving school spoke for themselves.

My mother dealt with the Second World War in only a few paragraphs. Nevertheless, this very brief section gives a vivid picture of what she experienced during her two-year period of war work.

---

[52] I first heard the term "creative non-fiction" coined by Andy Conway, author and time-traveller, when he applied the term to *There Was A Soldier*.

My mother merely mentions that she fainted on her first day, giving me ample scope to dramatise this incident.

I do not reveal the name of the factory where my mother worked on the grounds that the incidents imagined did not take place there. The scene that shows the swapping of completed work between my mother and Molly is purely imagined; the one where a woman gets her hair caught in a lathe took place in a similar factory on the outskirts of London. I merely borrowed this incident and placed my mother at the centre of it in her place of work.

Whilst my mother wrote very little about the Second World War, it was enough for me to enact, enhance and expand her experience as a war worker to develop twelve chapters (of nineteen), making her war work and her brief marriage the central act of the story.

There *was* an actual "mock invasion of Ecclefechan": it is mentioned only briefly in the memoir. During the mock exercise, my mother merely states that she met Harry Etheridge. However, my mother does not give any details how she met him or how long they knew one another before they married during the war. She merely states (in a few sentences) that they met, married, and then Harry left her for another woman shortly after the end of the war. I used these bare facts to show what might have happened.

My mother left me with nothing to work with in terms of my father's character. She never talked about him and I didn't ask. His presence in the memoir is almost to the point of being mentioned in passing; his brief part in my mother's life was, of course, highly significant and consequential.

Perhaps Harry changed when he returned from his war service? Perhaps men and women took a chance on their futures during the war? My mother doesn't say, leaving me to speculate to create his character. The facts speak for themselves: my mother was very quickly left as a single parent while she was pregnant shortly after the war.

It is worth noting here that my mother maintained a long relationship with Harry's parents. I readily recall holidays in Hastings, staying at their bungalow in the town high above the shore.

The memoir goes into some detail about our life living with Dora Walker, an influential period in my mother's post-war life. She also has a good deal to say about the difficult period after she left Mrs Walker's employ, a period characterised by moving from place to place, moving me from school to school until she found a suitable home for us and a "normal", non-specialist school for me.

The key revelation about my mother's parentage is mentioned only in passing; she merely states that she was born in Glasgow, not where she thought she was born. She does not go any further than state the fact, leaving me to imagine the circumstances of this overwhelming discovery. She does, however, leave a single, tantalising clue: her age when she found out that David Muir was not her natural father. I used this to write the scene that shows when she found out and how she reacted.

There is no mention of David Muir's funeral in the memoir, although it took place within its time frame. It is for this reason that I created the scenes associated with her father's funeral.

Neither is her mother's funeral mentioned, but I decided not to include scenes that show her mother's passing or her funeral on the grounds that my grandmother's death fell just beyond the time frame of the memoir.

My mother's memoir lay hidden and unopened from sometime in 1980 until my wife found it after her death in August 2013. I will always wonder if she forgot about it or if she long held the notion in her mind that it would be discovered one day, its discovery leading me by the hand to its secrets and revelations.

My arm of the Muir family ends with me. We have no children with whom to share the extraordinary stories of Davey, Kate, and Jean Muir. Instead, I offer their remarkable stories to you, my valued reader.

Characters

Members of the Muir family

Jean Burnie Johnstone Etheridge is, of course, my mother, the central character.

David ('Davey') Muir My mother always regarded David Muir as her father, even though he was not her natural father.

Catherine ('Kate') Johnstone: my mother's mother.

Aunty Chrissie: Kate, my grandmother, had a sister called Christina, usually known as Teen. I don't remember much about her, although I came into contact with Teen during my childhood holidays to Ecclefechan. The character of Aunty Chrissie is loosely based upon Teen.

My mother's siblings, in descending order of age, born between 1914 and 1933.

Marion
Davie
Jean, my mother, born in 1917
Kathy
Diana ('Danny')
William
Betty
Angus
Hiddleston
Murray

The Etheridge family

Harry Etheridge, my father.

William Etheridge and Clara Etheridge, Harry's parents.

Other Real Characters

In order of appearance:

Sheila: a childhood friend.

My mother's un-named employees during her working life between leaving school and beginning her war work.

Dora Walker: one of five daughters of George Dixon (1820 – 1898), councillor then mayor of the city of Birmingham; Liberal Member of Parliament for Edgbaston; an advocate for education for all.

Miss Ludford: the headmistress of George Auden School.

I had a bus guide to escort me between Mrs Walker's house in Hintelsham Avenue and my first school, the George Auden School for partially sighted children. There is no record of her name in my mother's memoir.

All other characters are fictitious, principally my mother's workmates at the factory during the Second World War and, importantly, Molly, her instructor. In her memoir, my mother only makes passing reference to her digs in Birmingham. The character of her landlady is fictitious.

Acknowledgements

Reflections Through The Mist grew initially out of the research for *There Was A Soldier* and, latterly, the discovery of my mother's memoir in that an early draft of *There Was A Soldier* included my mother's story. I am greatly indebted to Andy Conway (co-founder of New Street Authors) for suggesting that I unbundle that draft and write two stories. This I did, with the result that the second story follows from where the first ends.

Thus, there is some overlap between research for *There Was A Soldier* and *Reflections Through The Mist*. Research for the latter focussed largely upon the Second World War.

Throughout the whole period of what I call "the Muir project" – i.e. researching, writing and self-publishing both books – very many individuals provided me with help, advice, and time to assist me in bringing both stories to fruition. I am greatly indebted to all of them for their willingness, kindness, selfless generosity and support. I have striven to mention them all in the sections that follow. If I have left anyone out, then I take full responsibility for my oversight.

First and foremost, a special expression of gratitude goes to my wife, Annette. Her unfailing love, support and encouragement throughout have kept me going, and her timely ideas have often helped to resolve stumbling blocks.

I am also very grateful to my mentors Andy Conway and David Wake, co-founders of New Street Authors. Their support, inspiring ideas and encouragement have made a significant contribution to the completion of the Muir Project.

Beta Readers

A particular thank you for my beta reader: my wife, Annette. Her comments and suggestions were critical to the evolution of the final draft.

Professional Editing

I am indebted, once again, to my wonderful editor, Sarah Abel. Sarah's meticulous editing has proved invaluable.

Cover Design

A special thank you to David Wake for the cover design, following advice from Andy Conway that led to its tone and content.

Family Recollections

My cousin, Peter McGeer, continues to be a reliable source of Muir family history: thank you again, Peter.

Ancestry Research

I am especially indebted to Peter Payne and to Wendy Whiteley for their work in investigating the Muir family tree, and to Gordon McPhail for his thorough search for information about Thomas McDermott.

Other Acknowledgements

I am also very thankful to my brother-in-law, Michael Jones, for his valuable input to the section concerning my mother's war work. Michael used his first-hand experience of working on the shop floor as an engineer to inform me about the kind of work and working conditions that my mother would have experienced. He wrote a short story that illustrated what her first days would have been like, how she would have learnt to operate a lathe and adapt to working in a factory. I drew upon Michael's story to solidify and support my research into women factory workers in the Second World War.

Research Notes and Historical Notes

As mentioned in the Coda earlier, most of the research for *Reflections Through The Mist* centred upon the Second World War, principally the blitz in Birmingham and recorded experiences of women war workers.

A very special thanks go to Henrietta Lockhart, Collections Officer at the Winterbourne Oral History Project at Winterbourne Gardens, the University of Birmingham. Henrietta very kindly provided me with access to several oral recordings and transcripts of interviews with workers at an armaments factory in the northern suburbs of Birmingham during the Second World War. These "histories", taken together with the references (see below) enabled me to piece together a realistic and detailed picture of my mother's two-year period as a factory worker.

Finally, but most importantly, I wish to make a very special acknowledgement to my mother. Without her notebook, this book would not have been written. Moreover, if it hadn't been for her endeavours to secure a suitable education for me, it is very unlikely that I would have followed a path into higher education as an undergraduate and a postgraduate student, then as a university lecturer. In short, my desire and ability to write when I retired from academic life would not have existed.

References

Sue Bruley (ed), Working for Victory, *A diary of life in a Second World War factory,* (The History Press, 2010).

David Harvey, *Birmingham Buses, Trams and Trolleybuses in the Second World War,* (Amberley Publishing, 2019).

Inez Holden, *Blitz Writing,* (Handheld Press Limited, 2019).

Jacky Hyams, *Bomb Girls, Britain's Secret Army: the Munitions Women of World War II,* (John Blake Publishing Ltd, 2013).

Andrew Maxam and David Harvey, *Images of England: Smethwick,* (The History Press, 2013).

Julie Phillips, *Birmingham At War 1939–1945,* (Pen & Sword Military, 2018).

Smethwick Heritage Centre Trust, *Smethwick's Industrial Heritage,* (Smethwick Heritage Centre Trust, 2008).

Neil R. Storey and Fiona Kay, *Women in the Second World War,* (Amberley Publishing, 2019).

Keith Turner, *Images of England: Central Birmingham 1920–1970,* (The History Press, 2017).

Brian Wright (compiler), *Birmingham Blitz: our stories,* (Brewin Books, 2014).

About the Author

Photograph by Gareth Davies

David Muir was born in Scotland in 1947 and attended a number of boarding schools in the English Midlands. After a spell trying to be a schoolteacher, he spent over twenty years as a lecturer in one of the new universities in the West Midlands region, where he wrote a number of technical books on computing. David retired in 2010; he spends time writing fiction, a blog and poetry. He lives with his wife in Solihull.

David Muir's website is: davidmuir.website

Reviews (*There Was A Soldier*)

… a gripping story of a fight for survival that seems unimaginable in the society we now live. It also keeps alive knowledge of the tragedy of The Great War …

… An outstanding story …

… A thought-provoking story that portrays both the predicament of a soldier as well as the effects a war can have on those left at home and not knowing the fate of a loved one …

… An emotional story tells not only of horrific conflict, fear, confusion, distrust and loss but also friendship, fortitude, respect and compassion …

… Once I got into the story, I found it hard to put down and now I have finished I miss it! A tribute to David's story telling skills …

Also by David Muir

Visions of Whereafter tells the story of one man's uplifting adventure among those who have passed on from this world.

Finding Sarah tells the story of a forbidden love affair and its consequences that unfold through several generations of a family.

Printed in Great Britain
by Amazon